Bette Barnett

Creating Steel Jewelry

Etching, Fusing, Keum Boo, Enameling, Stainless and More

ARTISAN
IDEAS

Published by Artisan North America Inc., 2024.
By Bette Barnett
Layout and cover design: Andrea James Blaho
Technical Consultant: Harold O'Connor
Copyright© Bette Barnett
ISBN: 9798987738948
Library of Congress Control Number: 2024936138
Printed in China.
Artisan Ideas is an imprint of **Artisan North America, Inc.**
Info@ArtisanIdeas.com

For a selection of reference books visit our website:
www.ArtisanIdeas.com.

Artisan North America
753 Valley Road
Watchung, NJ 07069-6120

Authors!

If you have an idea for a book please contact us at: Info@ArtisanIdeas.com.
We'll be glad to hear from you.

DISCLAIMER

TABLE OF CONTENTS

FOREWORD

by Peter Johnsson

The use of iron and gold is older than written history. Iron and gold are still crucial components in our most advanced technology. Both metals express anthropomorphic qualities when we recognize their characteristics in powerful manifestations of personal traits: *"an iron will"*, *"a heart of gold"*....

Bette Barnett's art brings the mythic past in touch with the present moment through her creative explorations of techniques and materials in jewellry as objects of power.

As makers, artisans and artists we often find ourselves returning to the familiar themes, techniques, and materials that have proven to be successful in the past. However, our secret garden may become barren by too much familiarity and repetition. The richest harvest tends to grow from seeds that are gathered in uncharted territory beyond the edge of our known world.

In this book Bette presents to us a travelogue for curious metal artists who want to explore new creative territories. A multitude of techniques is clearly detailed so that we may ourselves explore the beauty in the marriage between iron and gold. It is a grimoire for the artisan alchemists who want to manifest a "metalmorphosis" in their work.

"Peter Johnsson is a world-renowned swordsmith and one of the most influential artists working in this medium today. Between 1985 and 1989 Peter pursued a Master's Degree from the University of Arts, Craft and Design in Stockholm. Upon receiving his Masters, he began a decade long career as a professional illustrator and graphic designer. In 1999 Peter continued his training and completed a BA in decorative metalwork at Stenebyskolan Academy of Design and Crafts, at the University of Gothenburg. Over the course of the last 20 years Peter has worked internationally as an artist and exhibition curator. His reconstructions of historical swords, edged tools and weapons are on display in European museums and private collections." — **Brett Holster**.

You can admire Peter Johnsson's work at: https://swordreflections.com

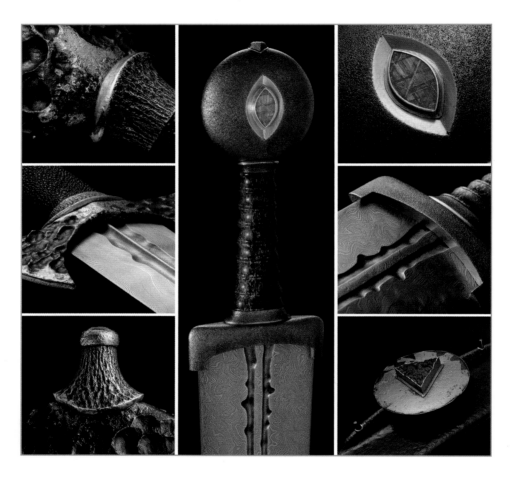

Two swords from the 2020 exhibition *Reflections—Dedication to the Goddess*, at Holster Fine Art, New York. The left-hand column shows details of the sword dedicated to Mnemosyne (goddess of memory), the center and right-hand columns show details of the sword dedicated to Asteria (goddess of falling stars and dreams).
Top left: pommel in iron with fused gold and upper grip ferrule in cast sterling silver with Keum Boo gold on the rim.
Middle left: guard of forged and carved steel with fused gold.
Bottom left: top of pommel with fused gold on rivet washer and Keum Boo on the cast silver rivet block.
Centre: Asteria sword, with blade of pattern welded steel, guard and pommel of forged and textured steel and grip of mineralized rib from a Steller's Sea Cow (now extinct).
Top right: detail of pommel with meteorite iron set in 24k gold on countersunk bevels with Keum Boo gold.
Middle right: detail of guard with Keum Boo gold. Grip ferrule with Keum Boo on the rim.
Bottom right: scabbard mounting for belt attachment. Shield of forged and textured iron with Keum Boo gold and a moldavite stone set in 24k gold.

INTRODUCTION

DESPITE ITS HUMBLE REPUTATION, STEEL offers a rich creative potential for metalsmiths. As a non-traditional material for jewelry, steel invites exploration and gives jewelers and other metal artists the opportunity to work with a common metal, and by applying vision, design, and skill, elevate it to art.

Steel also offers practical advantages for metalsmiths, not the least of which are cost and accessibility. Steel is strong, malleable, and ductile, making it workable and durable. It is lightweight, making larger pieces of jewelry comfortable and practical. Topping the list of advantages is steel's high melting temperature of approximately 2600°F (1427°C). This characteristic makes steel ideal for fusing non-ferrous metals to it because the vast majority have lower melting temperatures, including gold (1948°F/1064°C), silver (1763°F/962°C), copper (1983°F/1084°C) and their alloys.

Fusing gold and other non-ferrous metals to steel takes it to another level and results in jewelry that has a modern, gritty edge but which also feels ancient and rich. The tension created through the juxtaposition of noble and base metals has a surprising, almost paradoxical effect, setting off a visual vibration that is somewhat discordant yet alluring, weighty yet playful, earthy yet sophisticated. The counterpoint of the rich golden-yellow glow of gold against the jet black of patinated steel sets off some sort of primal whisper that murmurs, "*Yes, this is it. This is the proper balance of tension and beauty.*"

Gold and other non-ferrous metals can be combined with steel in many ways, giving metal artists the flexibility to try a range of creative possibilities and increase the caché of the resulting work. Simply put, adding gold and other metals to steel takes it from "crass" to "class."

Steel, though commonplace, can be turned into dramatic jewelry, particularly with the addition of fused gold. Renewal Cuff. Steel with fused 18k gold. Bette Barnett, 2020.

Objectives of this Book

My overarching goal for this book is to educate metal artists about working with steel so that the techniques described here continue to be applied and expanded. In short, I hope to help steel jewelry thrive and to promote continued interest in it for further exploration. To achieve that goal, I have written this book as an accessible, practical how-to guide for creating steel jewelry.

Each technique covered in this book is broken down into step-by-step processes, supported by photographs and illustrations. I hope that you will use the book as a benchtop guide to carry you through the process of making steel jewelry. Above all, my wish is that you enjoy getting your hands dirty working with steel and, through persistence and artistry, make the techniques your own.

Intended Audiences

This book is intended for jewelers who wish to expand their working knowledge of steel as a productive material, as well as blacksmiths and bladesmiths who are curious about venturing into a new area for their talents. While the processes described in this book are explained from the jeweler's perspective, I hope the information helps open a bridge whereby blacksmiths, bladesmiths and jewelry artists can begin to share some of their common body of knowledge about this amazing material and expand the knowledge on all sides.

With this book, I also hope to stimulate interest in steel jewelry among artists and art patrons, to move this type of work into the mainstream by creating awareness of the opportunities that exist for artists to exploit the many benefits of steel. Finally, I hope to inspire new ideas and spark creative explorations in steel jewelry.

My Perspective

My passion for steel jewelry dates to 2013 when I began taking workshops in steel and gold from Chris Nelson, a jewelry artist who was instrumental in introducing the process of fusing gold to steel in the United States. Before his death in 2017, Chris had taught many workshops across the country and inspired artists to begin working in steel and gold. Chris was strongly influenced in his work by Daniel Brush, whose multi-disciplinary art spans four decades and whose work in steel and gold stands in a class alone.

In 2014 Chris presented a paper to the Santa Fe Symposium® (SFS) entitled "*Iron Mused/Gold Fused…The New Iron Age*" in which he described his research into working with steel and fused gold.[1] Chris established and documented information and processes which included the preferred types of steel, effective gold alloys for fusing to steel, flux for protecting the steel during heating, and acid for dissolving oxides. In addition, his SFS paper covered many essential details including sourcing steel, hot vs. cold working, cutting, texturing, soldering, using a trinket kiln to enhance the fusing process, masking areas where gold is not desired, layering different alloys on steel and finishing steel jewelry.

In my first workshop with Chris, I was immediately enamored of the beauty of steel and gold and the creative possibilities afforded by steel. I continued to study through advanced workshops in steel, further deepening my interest in this area. After Chris' death in 2017, I kept exploring and developing new techniques to create steel mixed-metal jewelry and began offering workshops to share the body of knowledge.

In 2022 I presented a paper to the SFS entitled "*Steel Jewelry — New Horizons with Steel and Gold*", which built on Chris' research.[2] My paper provided new information on a number of topics related to creating steel jewelry including the range of different non-ferrous metals and alloys that can be successfully fused to steel, the use of alternative forms of steel such as wire and perforated steel sheet, **Keum Boo** on steel, fusing powdered

Group of steel and gold pieces featured in Chris Nelson's 2014 paper for the Santa Fe Symposium entitled "*Iron Mused/Gold Fused...The New Iron Age.*" Courtesy of Santa Fe Symposium.

metals to steel, the impact of various types of torches/gases on fusing and greater detail on the patinas and sealers that can be used successfully for steel. With permission from the SFS, my research paper has served as the foundation for this book. I am grateful to the Symposium for their support and generosity in permitting me to adapt my paper for the publication of *Creating Steel Jewelry*.

I have written this book from the perspective of a practical hands-on jeweler, not as a scholar or metallurgist, which I am not. I base my observations on my work since 2013 creating mixed-metal jewelry with steel. As with any technique, different artists have different processes and approaches to creating jewelry with steel. I am sharing the ones that have been most successful in my work. When appropriate, I have sought input from experts in metallurgy on specialized techniques involving steel and have referenced their contributions.

Dare to Be Different

Jewelers today typically work with silver and gold, which are referred to as **noble metals** because they resist oxidation and corrosion. Historically, the high market value of jewelry made of gold, silver and other noble metals such as palladium and platinum has been attributed to certain characteristics, such as color, luster, durability and malleability. The lower market value of jewelry made of base metals such as copper and iron has been attributed to the fact that they more readily oxidize and corrode. Thus, the term noble metals has become synonymous with value and expense and **base metals** associated with cheapness and low quality. In my view, these perceptions are out-of-step with the times.

The cost of noble metals has risen to the point that many metalsmiths, both beginners and veterans, cannot always afford using them for creative exploration and expression. As the late John Cogswell reminds us in his book *Creative Stonesetting*, precious metals *"are simply the materials with which we work. The price we pay to procure them is simply the cost of doing business."*[3]

As a non-traditional material, steel offers a rich repository of advantages for jewelers and other metal artists. It has the hardness, strength, springiness, durability, and malleability that we need. It is readily available and relatively cheap. But it also has another big advantage—it's different!

Cogswell points out, *"Jewelry created from alternative materials stands apart from more commonly employed silver and gold."* He goes on to add, *"When you create something that makes passers-by look twice, that can be a good thing. Dare to stand apart and try new things."*[4] As an alternative material, steel can serve as a catalyst that opens the floodgates of creativity. My hope is that by learning the techniques for working with steel that are described in this book you will also gain the freedom and confidence to dare to be different.

Presenting my paper to the 34th and final Santa Fe Symposium May 22–23, 2022 held at the Hotel Albuquerque in New Mexico.

1. BASICS OF STEEL

STEEL IS A COMMON THREAD that runs through our entire infrastructure. Think about it, we are surrounded by steel. Whether you're in your studio, workshop, home or car, steel is all around. From the structure of vehicles to the framework of furniture, to refrigerators and food cans in the grocery store, steel is ubiquitous.

Steel begins as iron ore, which is the second most abundant metal ore on earth, comprising 5.6 percent of the earth's crust (after bauxite, which comprises 8.2 percent and is used to produce aluminum). Iron is a silver-colored metal that conducts heat and electricity, though not as well as many other metals. One of iron's identifying characteristics is that it is strongly magnetic, which makes it easy to distinguish from other silver-colored metals.

Iron occurs naturally as ore, with the principal ones being hematite (ferric oxide, Fe_2O_3) and limonite (hydrated iron III) oxides-hydroxides, typically written $FeO(OH) \cdot nH_2O$. Other ores include siderite (ferrous carbonate, $FeCO_3$), taconite (an iron silicate) and magnetite (ferrous-ferric oxide, Fe_3O_4), which often occurs as a white sand.

Hematite is an iron ore and one of the most abundant minerals found in rock formations around the world. It often has a red color and so it is commonly used in pigments. Hematite has only a weak magnetic response and, unlike magnetite, is not noticeably attracted to an ordinary magnet.

Limonite, another common iron ore, is often used as a brown earth pigment and, in ancient times, was used as ornamental stone for small carved items such as beads and seals. It has been mined to produce iron for at least 2500 years.

Carbon Steel

By adding carbon and other alloying materials to iron, the result—steel—can be made a thousand times stronger and much more durable than iron alone. One of the main categories of steel is **carbon steel**, which is produced from **virgin steel**, **recycled steel** or both.

Virgin carbon steel is made by combining iron ore, **coke** (produced by heating coal in the absence of air) and lime in a blast furnace at around 3000°F (1650°C). The molten iron is alloyed with carbon from the burning coke. Impurities, called **slag**, float to the top and are removed. The molten steel contains roughly 4 percent carbon, which is then reduced by decarburization, which involves passing oxygen through the molten metal to oxidize the excess carbon. Most carbon steel alloys contain 1.5 percent carbon or less; beyond 2.1 percent carbon, the alloy is considered **cast iron**, which is harder and more brittle than lower carbon steels.

Steelmaking and the Environment

Steel is one of the most common metals. It is also 100 percent recyclable.

As an industry, steelmaking has a mixed impact on the environment. Steel production creates high carbon emissions, and the industry is actively seeking ways to reduce its carbon footprint including carbon capture and the use of green hydrogen rather than carbon.* While steel production results in high levels of greenhouse gases, steel is also the most frequently recycled material on the planet, somewhat offsetting its harm to the environment. In North America almost 69 percent of all steel is recycled— more than paper, aluminum, plastic, and glass combined. More than 95 percent of the water used for making steel in North America is also recycled.[5] In addition, recycled steel maintains all the properties of virgin steel, with large energy and cost savings versus mining and processing ore for new steel.

Evolution of Steel

Archeologists believe that ancient Egyptians discovered iron in the form of meteorites sometime between 5000 and 3000 BC and used it to make tools, weapons and trinkets. Evidence of the earliest known production of steel has been found in ironware from Anatolia (now the Asian portion of Turkey) that is nearly 4000 years old and dates from 1800 BC.[6]

As iron tools and weapons began to replace those of bronze, the Iron Age began its transition across the world in stages, beginning in the ancient Near East in the 12th century BC and then spreading throughout the Mediterranean into Asia and finally to Europe by about 500 BC.[7] During these ancient times, small amounts of iron ore were smelted by heating them in a charcoal fire and forge-welding the clumps together to force out impurities. When ancient man smelted iron in this manner, the result was an unintended "happy accident" in the history of metals. The use of charcoal to heat the iron released carbon, which alloyed with the iron to create a rudimentary form of steel.

During these early experiments, people did not understand the concept of alloying iron with carbon and simply believed they were using fire to create a purer form of iron. It wasn't until 1789 that carbon was identified as a chemical element and during that century scientists began to unlock the secrets of alloying metals. In the 1850s and 1860s, the Bessemer and Siemens-Martin processes turned steelmaking into the heavy industry that we know today.

*As of 2020 it is estimated that, in the USA, the steel industry was responsible for 7 to 9 percent of all direct fossil fuel greenhouse gas emissions.

Low Carbon Cold Rolled Steel

The World Steel Association lists more than 3,500 grades of steel with different physical, chemical and environmental properties. It's not surprising then that metal artists often find it confusing to source the proper type of steel for their work.

I prefer to use **low carbon steel** (often referred to as **mild steel**) because it is soft enough to be worked yet strong enough to be durable. Low carbon steel contains between .05 percent and 0.3 percent carbon.

Low carbon steel comes in both **cold rolled** and **hot rolled** finishes. During the finishing process, carbon steel is **annealed** and rolled into sheets. **Cold rolled steel** goes through an added step and is rolled again after it is cooled. This step results in steel sheet that has a smoother finish, greater durability and tighter tolerances than standard hot rolled mild steel, making it preferable for creating steel jewelry.

Low carbon steel is so versatile that it is used in a vast number of products, including household items, semi-permanent structures, fencing and more. It is also used for many common items such as cooking sheets and pizza pans, vent pipes and more. These all can be recycled and used for making jewelry. Got an old pizza pan? Simply clean, cut and flatten.

Although I work almost exclusively with low carbon cold rolled steel, some artists prefer stainless steel, which resists rust and corrosion, is strong and sustainable, and has a bright durable finish. However, stainless steel presents certain challenges, such as its fire and heat resistance, which must be considered when using it to create jewelry (see chapter 3).

Cold rolled low carbon steel has a smoother finish, greater durability and tighter tolerances than hot rolled low carbon steel.

Hot rolled low carbon steel has a rougher surface and is usually cheaper than cold rolled low carbon steel. It is not recommended for jewelry.

Historically, an ongoing demand for mild steel has meant high production volume and low costs. However, in recent years embargo taxes on steel imports, supply chain interruptions, and import restrictions have increased costs.

Hardness of Low Carbon Steel

Low carbon steels are softer and have less strength than higher carbon steels. However, low carbon steel is still a lot harder than non-ferrous metals that are commonly used for jewelry, including gold and silver.

You may be familiar with the Mohs scale, which was created in 1812, and is often used to rank the hardness of gemstones from 1 to 10 using a scratch test. When precision is needed to measure how well metals perform in an industrial setting, most metallurgists feel that the Mohs scale is not exact enough and instead use the Rockwell Hardness or the Vickers Scale. But when we are dealing with metals used for creating jewelry the Mohs scale is the most easily understood method to provide broad comparisons of hardness.

On the Mohs scale, carbon steels score from 4 to 6. Fine silver and gold score 2.5 to 5 and because of their softness are usually alloyed with other metals to increase their hardness and durability. Copper, brass and bronze score a 3, palladium a 4 to 4.5, platinum a 4.75 and titanium a 6. Chromium is the hardest pure metal known with a Mohs rating of 8.5.[8] What this comparison means for metal artists is that low carbon steel is about twice as hard as unalloyed silver and gold, but it is still soft enough to be effectively formed and worked.

Grades of Low Carbon Steel

The **SAE** steel grades system is a standard alloy numbering system maintained by SAE International (formerly the Society of Automotive Engineers), a U.S. professional standards organization for engineering professionals. In the 1930s and 1940s, the American Iron and Steel Institute (**AISI**) and SAE each had a numbering system for steel, but the two systems overlapped, so in 1995 the AISI turned the system over to SAE.

Today steel grades may refer to either or both SAE and AISI. Carbon steels are designated with a four-digit number where the first number is the main alloying ingredient (1 indicates carbon), the second number indicates major secondary elements (0 indicating none) and the last two numbers indicate the percentage of carbon in hundredths of a percent. For example, SAE/AISI 1010 steel is plain carbon steel with 0.10 percent carbon. The most common grades of low carbon steel are SAE/AISI 1008,1010, 1018, and 1020.

You may also see a reference to an **ASTM** grade. The ASTM system (maintained by The American Society of Testing and Materials) provides a quality measure of the safety and reliability for the metal. A36 is a low carbon steel that has small amounts of other alloying elements, such as manganese, sulfur, phosphorus, and silicon, to meet specific standards to make it suitable for structural applications, such as bridges, oil rigs, and parking garages to boat ramps and simple walkways.

Measuring Thickness of Low Carbon Steel Sheet

Low carbon steel sheet comes in a wide range of thicknesses, which are measured and sold in millimeters, fractional inches and occasionally **gauges**. Blacksmiths, bladesmiths and metal sculptors in the USA commonly refer to thicker steel by the fractional inch. The supplier that I use offers sheets ranging from 8 to 26-gauge.

Ferrous and non-ferrous metals of the same gauge have different thicknesses, and different gauge tools are used to measure them. Gauges for steel are slightly thicker than gauges for non-ferrous metals as shown in the table (next page). So, for example, if you want to work with steel sheet that approximates 18-gauge silver (1.02 mm), you might want to use 20-gauge steel (0.91 mm) as it is closer in thickness.

Standard gauge tool for measuring ferrous metals.

Ferrous and Non-Ferrous Sheet Metal Thickness				
	Ferrous Metals		Non-Ferrous Metals	
Gauge	Inches*	mm**	Inches*	mm**
8	.164	4.55	.128	3.26
10	.135	3.42	.102	2.59
12	.105	2.66	.081	2.05
14	.075	1.90	.064	1.63
16	.060	1.53	.051	1.29
18	.048	1.21	.040	1.02
20	.036	.91	.032	.81
22	.030	.76	.025	.64
24	.024	.61	.020	.51
26	.018	.45	.016	.41
28	.015	.39	.013	.32

*rounded up to the nearest .000
**rounded up to the nearest .00

For most of my work, I prefer 20-gauge low carbon steel, which is 0.036-inch or 0.91 millimeter. For pieces that require more heft, I will select 18-gauge, or for earrings and other pieces that need to be lighter or for layered pieces I might use 22 or 24-gauge. When selecting the thickness of metal, keep in mind that mild steel weighs about 25 percent less than silver, offering opportunities for creating larger pieces that remain comfortable to wear. This is a particular advantage for earrings.

> **Safety alert**: Avoid **galvanized steel** because it is coated with zinc to prevent rusting and corrosion. The zinc layer could be removed with heat, but the resulting zinc oxide fumes are toxic and can cause what is commonly called "fume fever", a condition that produces flu like symptoms. You can recognize galvanized steel by its slightly frostier, lighter appearance and granier surface texture.

Shopping for Low Carbon Steel Sheet

Whether you shop for steel at a local metal shop, hardware store or online metal vendor, it's a good idea to know in advance exactly what you need. The good news is that cold rolled steel is very common. In fact, you can often find it in hardware stores, but it may not be the thickness you want and cutting services are not usually available there.

Brick and mortar metal supply stores are usually great resources for buying low carbon steel, and they are fun places to browse. It's a good idea to search for local metal shops before shopping online because they allow you to look at available metals and ask questions. Also, most shops have metal cutting services enabling you to buy a convenient size of sheet for your needs. Often stores will have a drop or remnant section with odd pieces at bargain prices. Knowledgeable staff members can be a valuable resource for answering questions and giving advice. Simply specify that you want low carbon cold rolled steel (sometimes just called mild steel).

The store where I buy my steel sheet prices it by the pound, which is quite a treat if you're accustomed to buying metals by the ounce or pennyweight. Although mild steel is a bargain compared to non-ferrous metals, the costs have increased significantly in the past few years.

Metal supply stores usually have huge inventories of industrial metals and will cut the steel down to size if you wish.

Online suppliers are another good source for buying low carbon cold rolled steel. Be forewarned though that most metals websites list huge inventories of products and pinpointing exactly what you need can be challenging. Often online metal suppliers provide a metal worksheet, allowing you to fill in the exact specifications for your needs. With many variables listed including type of metal, physical form (sheet, rod, tube, perforated, etc.), sheet thickness (often shown in all measures of gauges, fractional inches and millimeters), dimensions and tolerance ranges, the inventory charts can be overwhelming. My recommendation is to be prepared with the specifications for your needs and use the site's search function and/or metals worksheet to narrow your choices. I have had great success just picking up the phone and calling a supplier if I need clarification on what to order. Keep in mind that shipping costs will be added to your order, and I have seen broad variability in these amounts.

Most metal supply stores and online suppliers require a minimum purchase, with the width and length usually specified in multiples of 12-inches. For example, common dimensions are 36 in. x 96 in., or 48 in. x 144 in., and often 24 in. x 24 in. is the smallest sheet size available. Some online suppliers and most storefront suppliers will cut sheets into workable sizes for a fee.

Physical Forms of Mild Steel

In addition to sheet, other physical forms of mild steel are available and offer significant design opportunities for jewelry. These include annealed steel wire, perforated steel sheet and steel mesh, each of which can serve as a foundation for fused metals.

Black Annealed Steel Wire

I often use black **annealed** steel wire, sometimes called **binding** or **baling wire** (aka **bale wire**), in my designs. It is commonly available from hardware stores and other suppliers. The wire comes annealed and coated with oil to help prevent rust. I clean the coating before working with the wire but some other artists do not find this step is needed. I remove the coating by scrubbing it off with pumice cleaner, otherwise it can be burned off with a torch and placed in an acid pickle bath. Gold and other metals can be readily fused to steel wire.

Safety alert: Don't use galvanized steel wire because of the danger of toxic fumes.

Steel wire offers a huge range of possibilities for jewelry. Brenda Schweder in her 2008 book *Steel Wire Jewelry: Stylish Designs, Simple Techniques, Artful Inspirations* provides information on the history and characteristics of steel wire plus a myriad of steel wire projects.[9]

Perforated Steel Sheet

Low carbon steel is also available as perforated sheet which comes in many patterns such as circles, diamonds, squares and honeycomb shaped openings. All low carbon steel perforated sheets can be fused with gold and other metals.

Expanded Steel Sheet

Expanded steel is sheet that has been cut and then stretched on an **expander** to produce a diamond pattern. It is available in many different sizes.

Woven Steel Mesh

Woven steel mesh, often referred to as **metal cloth**, offers many opportunities for steel jewelry. It is available in a range of sizes, based on the thickness of the wire, the number of wires per inch, and the size of the openings. The ability to form mesh into complicated dimensional shapes is one of its biggest advantages and makes mesh particularly adaptable for layered work. Gold and other metals and alloys can be fused to the coarser mesh sizes; however, the finer ones require careful torch control to avoid melting the steel wires. In addition, steel mesh poses other challenges including edge finishing and effective soldering.

History of Iron and Steel Jewelry

Many historians believe that the Hittites or Ancient Egyptians, who discovered iron in the form of meteorites somewhere between 5000 and 3000 BC, called it the *metal of heaven*. Thus began iron's long history as a sacred substance with magical powers. Early Egyptians placed iron in the mouths of mummies in the "*opening of the mouth*" ceremony, a ritual performed so that the deceased could eat and drink in the afterlife.

Examples of iron jewelry have been traced to as early as 3000–2000 BC. These early forms of iron jewelry signified status. Throughout the period 2000–1900 BC, iron was treated as a luxury material like gold. However, by the 10th century BC, iron was regarded as utilitarian and was commonly used for weapons and tools instead of ornamentation.

Iron jewelry from ancient times is scarce. Before the start of the Iron Age in roughly 1200 BC, production of iron jewelry was limited. This is because the ancients had not yet discovered the **casting** process and could only smelt it—heat it to a semi-molten state. Thus they were able to hammer and pound it to create tools and weapons. But in this semi-molten state it was hard to form and became brittle when cold, so the smelting process was rarely used for non-essential items.

After Chinese metallurgists developed a process for casting iron around 645 BC, the creation of

An ancient iron fibula/pin dated 450–1 BC found in a grave in the Czech Republic. Courtesy of the Penn Museum, object #29-29-26.

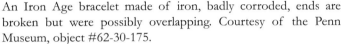

An Iron Age bracelet made of iron, badly corroded, ends are broken but were possibly overlapping. Courtesy of the Penn Museum, object #62-30-175.

An Iron Age anklet made of iron found in a burial cave in Jordan. Courtesy of the Penn Museum, object #81-6-53.

decorative objects such as jewelry became more common. However, because iron quickly oxidizes and corrodes, much of the iron jewelry from those times has failed to survive and many items that have been discovered were so degraded as to be unidentifiable. Most iron jewelry from the Iron Age that did survive is in the form of thick large rings such as bracelets or anklets.

Citizens of the early Roman Empire wore only iron jewelry because gold was outlawed for a time. Even senators and other officials wore iron and switched to gold only when they represented Rome in an official capacity. Ancient Greeks were obsessed with hematite, one of the major iron ores, and they named it Haima, which is the ancient Greek word for blood. They wore iron rings to symbolize strength. In the early Greek Church, the bride received an iron ring while the groom received a ring of gold. Later in Greece iron became a sign of slavery.

Scholars believe that certain early African cultures reinforced the mystical qualities of iron jewelry by wearing it as a talisman for protection against evil. This jewelry often contained potions to increase its magical power. In Benin, in West Africa, from the 1400s through the 1800s, iron alloys were used for pendants and simple jewelry. Ancient Arabians also wore iron charms, often with inscriptions of intent.

The mystical quality of iron jewelry also can be traced to Europe where iron was commonly made into charms to protect against evil spirits, impart physical strength, heal illness, or even make the wearer invisible. In Ireland iron was placed in a baby's bed to prevent kidnapping by the fairies, and in Scotland fishermen touched iron as a protective talisman, a practice that continues to this day. In Scotland after a death, pieces of iron were put into food and drink to block the devil from entering them.

Iron jewelry appeared in France in the mid-18th century, when King Louis XV encouraged wealthy citizens to "donate" their precious gems and metals to pay for military campaigns during the Seven Years War, a major conflict between Great Britain and France lasting from 1756 to 1763. As gold and silver adornments were donated, iron jewelry became popular. In Paris after the 1789 Storming of the Bastille and destruction of the infamous prison, revolutionaries pillaged the rubble for metal and rock as souvenirs. Old iron prison bars were removed and used to make rings, many with the word "Bastille" inscribed. Other jewelry pieces bore inscriptions reading *Liberte Française 14 Juillet* (*French Liberty 14 July*). Bastille iron jewelry remained popular through the end of the 18th century.

In Berlin during the 1790s cast iron jewelry was introduced as mourning jewelry because the delicate **open work** of the jewelry and its black **matte** finish gave it a restrained appearance. At that time, this jewelry was seen as rather boring, but that changed when in 1813–1815 the royal Prussian family required citizens to contribute gold and silver to fund the revolution against Napoleon. In exchange, people received Berlin iron jewelry often inscribed with *Gold gab ich für Eisen* (*I gave gold for iron*). As a result, during the Napoleonic wars, Berlin iron jewelry became a symbol of patriotism and honor. Over time, the jewelry's popularity increased due to its beautifully detailed craftsmanship and matte lacquer coating. In England in the period 1811–1820 when the Prince of Wales served as Regent, Berlin iron jewelry became even more popular and became known across the Continent.

In the U.S. Alexander Calder, the artist who popularized the mobile, worked extensively with steel, making hundreds of interactive, mechanical circus figures from it. His innovative use of industrial materials such as steel represented a fresh approach that helped pave the way for new perceptions in the art world about the value of jewelry art. In the 1940s and 50s he made many pieces of unconventional hammered wire jewelry from steel and other metals without any soldering involved and established a precedent in the U.S. for using steel in fashionable jewelry.

Berlin iron jewelry is distinctive because of its delicate openwork and matte black finish. Metropolitan Museum of Art.

Alexander Calder's innovative steel jewelry prompted new perceptions about fashion jewelry. Alexander Calder cuff circa 1940.

In addition to its mystical properties, iron has long been associated with the planet Mars because its crust is rich in iron. In fact, oxidation of iron in the planet's crust is what causes its red color. Mars represents male energy, and by association, iron jewelry has symbolized classically male characteristics of strength, tenacity, fortitude, honor and confidence. Consider Margaret Thatcher, the "Iron Lady", who epitomized these traits because of her uncompromising and persistent leadership style.

Today, across the globe, iron jewelry is worn as fashion and for symbolic purposes. Sikhs wear cast iron or steel bangles called *Karas* that symbolize commitment to their faith. These were originally used like brass knuckles in hand-to-hand combat to guard the sword arm of the Khalsa warriors. Today, Canadian engineers receive an iron or steel ring at graduation symbolizing their obligation to live by a high standard of professional conduct.

2. WORKING WITH LOW CARBON STEEL

THE LOW CARBON CONTENT OF mild steel makes it softer than other varieties of steel, meaning it's easier to cut, file and form. In addition, mild steel that is 16-gauge (1.53 mm) or thinner is malleable enough to be worked cold without the need of a forge or furnace.

Most of the usual jewelry making techniques can be applied to low carbon steel with little difference from working with non-ferrous metals. However, steel does present some key differences, which may take a bit of getting used to.

Rust—That Four-Letter Word

If you have avoided using steel as a material for jewelry because of problems caused by rust, you may want to reconsider because rust removal is simple, and preventing future rust on steel jewelry is easily achieved because of advances in metal sealers (see chapter 9).

Rust is an iron oxide caused by a chemical reaction between iron and oxygen, in the presence of moisture. I find rusted steel to be quite beautiful, but unsealed rusted jewelry that will be in contact with clothing or skin is a problem because it can stain or bleed. As rust develops, it is shed off the metal, exposing the underlying surface to more corrosion and eventually complete decay; not a good prospect for jewelry.

Rusted steel can be artistically pleasing but it can be a problem for jewelry.

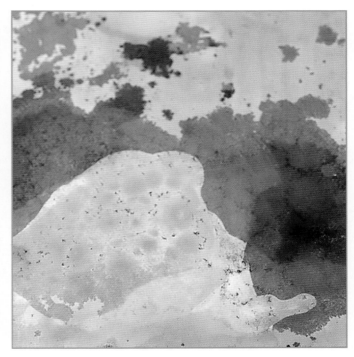

Modern products do a great job of removing rust. After rust removal, you may see a slight shadow left behind, which is not a problem.

Steel that has been stored for a while or newly cleaned steel is likely to develop rust, particularly in humid climates. Many rust removal products are available, and several of the ones I have used successfully are:

- **Vinegar**. Soak the metal in household white vinegar for about 30 minutes or more if the rust is heavy. Remove and scrub with pumice cleanser using a stiff brass brush or mesh scrub pad. Vinegar is non-toxic, environmentally friendly and inexpensive. Also, it can be reused for this purpose.

- **Evapo-Rust®**. This product is available commercially in many hardware stores and online. In a container, pour enough Evapo-Rust® to completely cover the rusted metal and leave it for 30 minutes for light rust or up to overnight for very heavy rust. Then rinse and wipe dry. Less scrubbing is required with the Evapo-Rust® compared to the vinegar. It is described on the label as being non-toxic.

- **Whink® Rust Stain Remover**. This commercially available rust remover is an industrial-strength product that utilizes aggressive acid to remove stubborn rust stains. It is extremely effective and begins working immediately to dissolve rust. Simply pour, spray or wipe it on and rub the rust off with a rag or brush.

> **Safety alert**: Although Whink® is very effective, you should be aware that it contains hydrofluoric acid, which is extremely corrosive. Be sure to wear protective gloves and eye wear and have good ventilation.

Once rust has been removed and the surface of the steel is clean, it will be highly reactive, making it even more susceptible to rust. Thus, it usually makes sense to delay rust removal until your work requires a clean surface, for example, before soldering or fusing metals to it.

Cleaning and Preparing Low Carbon Steel Sheet

Steel comes from the supplier coated with metal dust and possibly a film of oil. I store steel sheets in my studio as they come from the supplier. Then before starting any step that involves a surface treatment, such as soldering, fusing or Keum Boo, I remove any rust and clean the steel thoroughly.

When working with steel, it's important to keep it clean. Any dirt, oil, oxidation or **scale** can interfere with surface treatments. The steps that I recommend for cleaning low carbon steel are:

- **Using a pumice based cleanser scrub with a stiff brass brush**. Using a pumice-based cleanser, such as Bar Keepers Friend®, Fast Orange®, GoJo® or pumice powder, on a stiff brass brush, firmly scrub the metal and rinse until water sheets off the surface instead of forming droplets. This step removes any dirt and dust.

- **Roughen slightly with a woven mesh pad**. Use an all-purpose Scotch-Brite® mesh pad to scrub the surface in many different directions, raising roughness or tooth onto the surface. Metal surfaces may appear smooth, but at a microscopic level they have asperities or irregularities. Roughening the surface helps raise microscopic projections making the metal more receptive to surface treatments such as etching, soldering and fusing.

- **Wipe with a degreaser such as alcohol**. Wipe the surface with alcohol (denatured or isopropyl) or any quality degreaser to ensure there are no oils or fingerprints on the surface. Denatured alcohol is a form of ethanol (grain alcohol or drinking alcohol), referred to as "methylated spirits", which contains additives that make it non-drinkable. Isopropyl alcohol, often called rubbing alcohol, is a "surgical spirit" rather than a "methylated spirit" and consists of pure ethanol, usually at a concentration of 70 percent or 99 percent. Avoid using acetone as a degreaser because it leaves a residue that is hard to remove and may interfere with surface treatments.

Scrub the steel with pumice cleanser. If you see droplets of water on the surface, continue scrubbing.

Scrub the steel until water sheets off the surface.

Cutting and Sawing Low Carbon Steel Sheet

Shearing

Quality **bench shears** are effective for cutting mild steel sheet provided the shear is specified for such use. You can choose from two different types—a **throatless shear** or a **guillotine shear**. A throatless shear has two blades that converge at the throat in an acute angle. The shear is operated by pulling a diagonally raised handle forward and down, which lowers the top blade and cuts the metal. If the sheet is longer than the blades, it can be pushed past the angle, continuing the cutting process. Typically, the maximum thickness that can be cut by a throatless shear is 18-gauge (1.214 mm), so you should check the rating before purchasing one. Throatless shears are usually cheaper than guillotine shears and the blades can be made of different materials, including cast iron or high carbon steel, but rarely hardened tempered tool steel. The throatless shear differs from the guillotine shear in that it allows long pieces of metal to be fed through the blades as they are cut.

In addition, a throatless shear allows for curved cuts because the metal can be moved across the machine during the shearing process. The longer the blades, the more leverage is needed, which is increased by adding length to the handle.

Guillotine shears have upper and lower parallel blades that are often made of precision-ground hardened tempered steel. After positioning the metal against a holding tray for precise alignment, the metal is fed through the blades, which are then closed by pulling the handle forward and down.

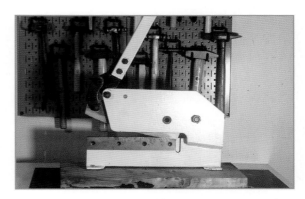

Throatless shears are often less expensive than guillotine shears and allow more versatility regarding the dimensions of the metal to be cut.

Guillotine shears allow for accurate, straight cuts, but cannot be used to cut curves.

Guillotine shears allow for very accurate, straight cuts; however, the dimensions of metal that can be cut are limited by the length of the blades, often 6 to 12-inches (15.2 to 30.5 cm). Be sure to consider the size of sheet that you will be cutting before choosing a shear.

Replacement blades are usually available for both types of shears.

Handheld Shears

Handheld shears are useful for cutting thinner metal or for small, more intricate cuts that cannot be achieved with a bench shear. Two types of useful handheld shears are **aviation snips** and **tin snips**. Aviation snips are best for making precise turns because of their spring-loaded design and the teeth on the blades, while tin snips are better for straight cuts through thinner metal. Tin snips have a standard scissor design and are easy to use for straight cuts, but they are not as powerful as aviation snips and can cause hand fatigue. Their blades are shorter than regular scissors and the handles are longer, which gives more cutting control. Both aviation and tin snips come in three different cut angles, and often the color of the handle will denote at what angle the snip cuts. Red handles create straight and left angle cuts, green handles create straight and right-angled cuts, and yellow handles create straight cuts with wide curves.

Goat and **sheep hoof trimmers** are extremely versatile for mild steel through 20-gauge (0.91mm). With straight pointed blades and easy-to-grip handles that are squeezed to close the blades. Hoof trimmers are useful for making short straight or curved cuts.

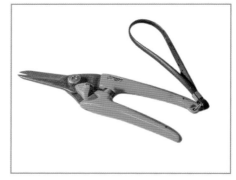

Aviation snips have a spring-loaded design and teeth on the blades, making them stronger and less tiring to use.

Tin snips are easy to use for straight cuts on thinner metals.

Goat hoof trimmers are extremely versatile and effective for short straight or curved cuts.

Power Tools for Cutting

Different types of power tools are useful for cutting low carbon steel. Two of the most common are **nibblers** and **power shears**. As nibblers cut through the metal, they remove some of it in the form small chips that fly everywhere, so they are not suitable for cutting extremely fine lines like hand shears or snips would.

Power shears come in single or double cut varieties. Single cut shears slice cleanly through sheet metal without creating any waste, though they usually distort the metal in the process. Single cut shears can handle thicker metals better than either nibblers or double cut shears. As their name implies, double cut shears have two cutting blades that remove a thin strip of material but leave minimum distortion if they are kept straight. Double cut shears are not great for curved cuts and not suitable for heavier duty applications for which single cut shears are better.

Power nibblers remove metal in the form of small chips that fly everywhere.

Single cut power shears cut without waste but cause some distortion.

Sawing

Sawing steel is similar to sawing non-ferrous metals but requires a bit more tenacity. Any quality jeweler's saw frame and blades will work for sawing low carbon steel, but saw blades designed for cutting platinum are extremely effective for steel and help make sawing easier and faster.

I use a 3/0 or 4/0 blade to saw steel sheet of 18 to 20-gauge (1.2 to 0.9 mm). For thinner gauges I use a 4/0 to 6/0 blade. I also use an electric mini bench saw to cut up to 18-gauge (1.2 mm) steel sheet saving considerable time, particularly when cutting curved shapes. To effectively cut low carbon steel, the bench saw that I use requires blades that are 0.1038-inch x 24 teeth-per-inch (TPI).

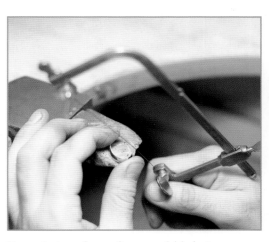

Using a lubricant (wax or oil) for sawing is a matter of preference. Many metal artists feel that a lubricant makes sawing smoother and helps keep the blade sharp. I prefer sawing without a lubricant because I find that helps me have a better feel for the blade moving through the metal.

Your choice of saw frame and blade is a matter of personal preference. However, saw blades designed for platinum are ideal for sawing low carbon steel.

Filing, Sanding and Polishing Low Carbon Steel

Filing and sanding mild steel is much the same as with non-ferrous metals. However, because of its hardness, steel often requires somewhat coarser files and abrasives to achieve desired results. I often use coarse grinding wheels and other abrasive wheels to remove burs before filing and sanding. I have a bench lathe with a large deburring wheel that makes quick work of removing burs from metal when needed. In addition, Scotch-Brite™ radial bristle discs and wheels, which are impregnated with a mineral abrasive, are very effective for smoothing the steel.

A deburring wheel is very useful for removing rough edges after sawing. This one is designed for a large bench lathe, but smaller wheels are available.

Low carbon steel doesn't require a lot of final polishing, particularly if the surface is to be patinated. I typically end the polishing process with a 400-grit radial wheel and possibly a final smoothing with a pre-polish compound such as Fabulustre Cut® or Polish Compound®. If you choose to leave the steel its natural color, it is possible to polish it to a high shine using polishing wheels and compounds designed for non-ferrous metals.

Soldering Low Carbon Steel

Low carbon steel can be soldered (technically it's brazing because of the higher temperature) using conventional jewelry soldering methods. Cold rolled steel can be soldered to itself or other metals, and various types of solder can be used. When soldering mild steel, it is critically important for the metal to be clean and the join perfectly aligned without gaps. Because steel is less conductive than non-ferrous metals, the **capillary effect**, where solder rapidly flows along a seam, is reduced and the solder tends to flow outward rather than along the seam of the join.

Tools and Supplies for Soldering

Torch. To solder steel, you will need to use a torch that can produce a very hot **oxidizing flame**. Dual gas (oxygen and either acetylene or propane) and acetylene/ambient air torches work well. However, torches that rely on MAPP gas, propane or butane are less effective.

Flux. When soldering, you should use flux to protect the steel against oxidation, which impedes the flow of solder. Any type of paste or liquid flux can be used, but I prefer a black brazing flux (Handy Flux B-1® or Stay-Silv® Black Hi-Temp Brazing) because it stays effective up to higher heat (1800°F/982°C) than regular white paste flux, which breaks down at about 1600°F (871°C). The black brazing fluxes contain hydrogen fluoride, which is corrosive and toxic but safe if you have good ventilation and avoid inhaling the fumes. Low carbon steel is not subject to firescale so there is no need to use a barrier flux.

Carbon steel oxidizes quickly and dramatically, so it is important for the heat to be high enough to melt the solder before a build-up of oxidation or scale can occur. I usually start with a neutral flame until the flux becomes sticky enough to hold the solder in place. Then I use a sharp oxidizing flame applied directly to the area of the solder join rather than circling my torch around to heat the entire piece.

Pickle. Pickle is the common name for a mild acid solution that is used to remove the oxidation from metals. Typical pickles used for this purpose include sodium bisulfate (marketed under different brand names including PhDown®), vinegar, a vinegar/salt combination and citric acid. I prefer sodium bisulfate, but it's really a matter of choice.

The pickle solution is more effective if it is warmed slightly to approximately 100° to 150°F (38° to 66°C). Crock pots are commonly used as pickle pots, but I find that they overheat the pickle solution, causing it to prematurely lose its effectiveness. Instead, I prefer to use a hotplate that can be set to a lower temperature with a heat-resistant non-reactive container and lid.

You will need to maintain a separate pickle container for steel (including steel mixed-metal pieces). If you comingle ferrous and non-ferrous metals in the same container, the non-ferrous metals will develop a layer of copper plating, which would need to be removed.

Copper plating is likely to occur with steel mixed-metal pieces as well, but it is easy to remove with a brisk scrub using a stiff brass brush. Otherwise you can simply mix up a batch of "super pickle", which is a half-

and-half solution of white vinegar and hydrogen peroxide three-percent solution. Place the copper plated piece into the solution. It will bubble as the copper is quickly dissolved from the surface. It's a single-use solution as the peroxide (H_2O_2) releases one of its oxygen molecules during the process, leaving a solution of vinegar and water, which can be poured into your pickle pot.

Copper plating is a common occurrence when ferrous and non-ferrous metals are combined in mixed-metal jewelry.

A super pickle solution of 50 percent household white vinegar and 50 percent hydrogen peroxide three-percent solution makes quick work of removing copper plating.

How to Solder Low Carbon Steel

1   **Prepare**. Prepare the steel by cleaning it thoroughly. Ensure the join is completely clean and well aligned with no gaps. File and sand the edges to be completely flat and flush against each other with no light showing through.

2   **Set up**. Set up the soldering operation so that the metal is well supported on a soldering surface. As an alternative, if you can support the pieces in a way that enables you to heat from below the metal, you will be able to use the heat to pull the solder through the join to the back, increasing the stability. You can use third hand locking tweezers or fire bricks for that purpose.

3   **Apply flux and place solder**. Apply flux to the area of the join. You do not need to spread the flux in a wider area. Place pieces of solder on the steel so they are in contact with both sides of the join. For ferrous metals, you will need to use somewhat more solder than for non-ferrous metals. You can use wire or chip solder, depending on your preference, or use pick soldering where you heat the join and your solder pick, which you will then use to pick up a ball of melted solder and place it directly on the join.

4   **Melt the solder**. Using a sharp oxidizing flame, place it near the join and move it back and forth gently until the flux becomes sticky and the pieces of solder stop moving. Then position the hottest part of the flame (just beyond the blue cone) directly on the seam and hold it until the solder flows. The key is to hold your torch close to the join rather than circle around as you would with non-ferrous metals. The steel may heat to a bright orange before the solder flows, but you don't need to be concerned that it will melt.

This same process should be used whether soldering steel to steel or non-ferrous metals to steel. However, if the join involves soldering a non-ferrous metal to steel, keep the heat focused on the steel and use its ambient heat to flow the solder. This will help to avoid melting the non-ferrous metal.

5 **Cool and quench**. After the solder has flowed, allow the steel to cool slightly at room temperature before **quenching** it in water. Steel will be a bit slower to cool than non-ferrous metals and if you move it too quickly the join is likely to break.

6 **Place the piece in the pickle**. After quenching, immerse the steel in the mild acid solution to remove oxidation. Steel oxidizes considerably more than non-ferrous metals and the oxidation is more difficult to remove, so you'll need to leave the metal in the pickle longer. With a fresh pickle solution, I usually check the metal after 15 minutes, remove and rinse it, and then give it a good scrub with pumice cleanser using a stiff metal brush to remove as much oxidation as possible. Then I place it back in the acid and repeat the process every 15 minutes until the metal is clean. It can take up to an hour or more to remove the oxidation.

Step 1–Set up the soldering operation by ensuring that the steel is clean, the edges are filed smooth and flat, and the join is perfectly tight, with no gaps.

Step 2–The soldering set-up is worth your time and attention. By supporting the piece from above, such as shown here with this ring supported by a third hand, it is possible to heat from below and pull the solder through the join, increasing its strength.

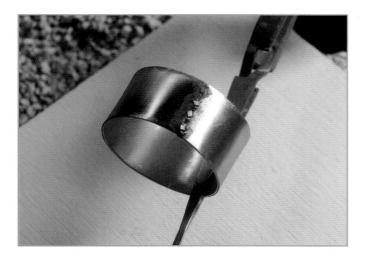

Step 3–Here the black brazing flux has been applied only to the area of the join. Because of steel's low conductivity, you should use slightly more solder and place it directly on the join. Pick soldering is another option.

Step 4–After using a neutral flame to get the flux tacky, move to an oxidizing flame focused directly on the join until the solder flows.

Step 5–Because steel cools more slowly than non-ferrous metals, allow a bit of time for it to air cool slightly before quenching. Note how heavily steel oxidizes.

Step 6–Oxidized steel requires more time in the acid solution than non-ferrous metals. After 15 minutes, remove and scrub it with pumice cleanser and a brass brush. Repeat until the oxidation is removed.

Completed solder join on low carbon steel–Note that the excess solder has been abraded off on one side but on the other some solder still needs to be cleaned off.

Disposing of Spent Pickle

Over time, the pickle solution will become cloudy and filled with bits of scale and oxidation. I often add a bit of acid to the solution to beef it up a bit, but at some point, it will simply stop working, and you will need to mix a fresh solution.

Don't pour spent pickle outside as the solution and metals in it can contaminate soil and ground water and are harmful to wildlife. I keep a large plastic paint bucket outside in the open air and cover it loosely with an old towel. I pour the acid into the bucket and let it collect until I have enough to dispose of it at a hazardous waste facility. Different facilities have different disposal rules, but in my locale we are required to place the solution in a sealed container, schedule an appointment and deliver it to the facility at the specified time.

Troubleshooting the Soldering Process

- **Solder Does Not Flow along the Entire Join**. The likely cause is that you did not use enough heat and excess oxidization built up to the point that it prevented the complete flow of the solder. Another cause may be an insufficient amount of solder. Pickle and clean the metal thoroughly, add flux and more solder and repeat the soldering process.

- **Solder Balls Up and Does Not Flow**. Insufficient heat is the likely culprit here. If the heat is too low, oxidation will form and the solder will simply ball up and refuse to flow. Pickle and clean the metal thoroughly. Some of the balls of solder may fall off when scrubbed. Apply more solder and repeat the soldering process.

- **Solder Flows away from the Join**. To flow and fill a join, the pieces of solder need to be placed so that they are touching both sides. Otherwise, the solder may refuse to flow into the join. If this occurs, you should pickle and clean the metal thoroughly, add flux and apply solder so that it touches both sides of the join. Repeat the soldering process.

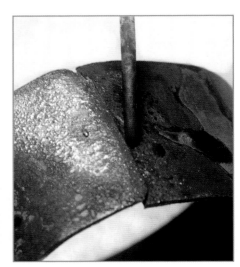

If the solder does not flow along the entire join, insufficient heat is the likely culprit.

When soldering, it is important to focus a hot oxidizing flame on the join to avoid excess oxidation, which can stop the solder from flowing and cause it to ball up.

If the solder is not touching both sides of the join, it may flow away from the seam.

Forming Low Carbon Steel

Low carbon steel is surprisingly malleable, meaning that at thinner gauges it can easily be hammered or formed without cracking. Steel is also quite ductile, meaning it can be stretched, shaped, or bent without fracturing. The process and tools used to form steel are identical to those for forming other metals; however, because steel is harder, the process may require a bit more force and perseverance. When it comes to forming, low carbon steel is a forgiving metal and does not show hammer marks as readily as non-ferrous metals.

Mild steel can be scored, bent, and folded in the same manner as other metals. However, because steel is harder than most other metals, thinner gauges work better for these processes.

Work Hardening and Annealing Low Carbon Steel

Mild steel comes from the supplier in an annealed state. Annealing gives the metal flexibility and annealed steel is ready to be formed. Low carbon steel almost never **work hardens**, which is a big advantage allowing you to work the metal extensively by hammering, rolling, drawing, or other physical processes without concern for it becoming too stiff.

With thinner gauges of mild steel (18-gauge or thinner) the metal almost never becomes stiff and difficult to form. Although rare, it is possible for low carbon steel to become work hardened, particularly at thicker gauges. In this case, the metal can be softened by heating it with a torch to a bright orange-red (not cherry red) and holding it there for a bit until you are certain that it is heated all the way through. Then place it in vermiculite or dry sand to slow the cooling process and better maintain the annealed state. This allows the metal to be soft enough to undergo further cold working without fracturing.

To a large extent the carbon content of steel determines whether it can be heat hardened. Low carbon steel does not have enough carbon to harden it thoroughly with heat.

However, if cooling is rapid enough, another method of hardening occurs—**carburizing**—also called **case hardening**. Carburizing is the process of using heat to diffuse carbon into the surface of low-carbon steels to increase hardness. The material is then quenched quickly so the carbon is locked in place. To case harden low carbon steel, it is first heated to a cherry red (above 1000°F/538°C) in the presence of carbon (such as ground charcoal) and kept at this constant temperature for at least a few minutes to diffuse carbon into the surface, and then the object is quenched in oil or water. Mild steels that have been carburized in this way have a hard surface and a soft core. This means that case hardened low carbon steels are harder but not brittle. The core is still ductile and strong while being better protected by the hard surface against wear and fatigue. Although case hardening is not necessary, it can help add strength and durability to pieces of jewelry. The case hardening process should be done after the work is fully formed but before any other heat processes are completed, such as fusing or soldering.

In the rare instance that low carbon steel becomes work hardened, you can soften it by simply heating it to an orange-red, then hold it for 10 to 12 seconds until it is thoroughly heated, and place it in vermiculite or sand to slowly cool.

Do You Need Separate Tools for Steel?

For many years I have used the same tools—bench shear, rolling mill, saws, files and hammers—interchangeably for both low carbon steel and non-ferrous metals without any damage to the tools. However, keep in mind that low carbon steel is about twice as hard as fine silver and gold. So over time, certain tools that are used repetitively, such as hammers, stamps and files can be dulled by use on steel. For example, I have a beautiful and expensive texturing hammer that has been flattened over the course of five years by use on steel. My advice is to use high quality hardened steel tools for striking or cutting implements such as stamps, disc cutters, shears, texturing hammers and chisels. Or, as an alternative, use cheaper softer steel tools that can be considered consumable items.

Title: Infinity Brooch.
Artist: Bette Barnett.
Description: Steel fused with several different powdered metals, including fine silver, brilliant bronze and 18k yellow gold. 2024.

3. WORKING WITH STAINLESS STEEL
by Andy Cooperman

Author's note: I met Andy Cooperman in April 2022 when attending one of his workshops called *Imaginative Captures*. I had read outstanding reviews of his teaching and had been following his work for years. Andy's uncanny ability to execute design from a totally fresh perspective, combined with his spot-on precision as a jewelry artist, resonated powerfully with me. After years of admiring Andy's work, I was not disappointed with the workshop. I came away feeling that I had gained a completely new perspective. I also came away with Andy's agreement to contribute a chapter to this book. I was delighted that a jeweler with his accomplishments had offered to share his knowledge in an area that is completely outside my skill set—stainless steel.

A metalsmith since 1980, Andy works from his Seattle studio where he builds jewelry and objects for exhibitions and private clients. His work and writing have appeared in blogs, magazines and books, including *Humor in Craft*, *Art Jewelry Today* (I, II & III) and *The Penland Book of Jewelry*, and is held in private and public collections such as the Victoria and Albert Museum, Central College in Pella Iowa, Goshen College, Indiana and the Tacoma Art Museum.

Here, he shares information on his experience with stainless steel, including its working characteristics and his approach to using it in his creations.

Website: www.andycooperman.com
Instagram: @a.cooperman

WHAT'S SO GREAT ABOUT STAINLESS steel? The name says it all….

Stainless steel is strong, lightweight, durable, tarnish free and corrosion resistant. In many ways a wonderful jewelry material. It can be forged, formed and fabricated with most of the tools at our benches. It can be cast using specialized equipment or sent out to casters that are equipped for it. It can be milled and machined. I use stainless when I need a metal that will retain its luster, like a reflector behind a translucent stone or object, or when I need a metal that will hold up in harsh environments. And stainless is inexpensive, which encourages play and experimentation.

In the 1800s researchers were looking for a steel that wouldn't corrode. Many contributed to the development of a "rustless" steel but it was a scientist from Sheffield, England named Harry Brearley who, on August 13, 1913, is credited with the invention of the stainless that we use today.

We all know what stainless steel is. But what *IS* stainless steel? Stainless steel (often marked SS or *stainless*) is a family of steel alloys that, like all steels, contain iron and a small amount of carbon. Stainless is actually a relatively soft metal but work hardens quickly, and depending on how it is treated in the factory or studio, can be very hard.

Harry Brearley understood that low carbon and higher amounts of chromium were the keys to producing a truly *stainless* steel. Modern stainless steels contain under 1 percent carbon and at least 10.5 percent chromium and, depending on the alloy, also contains nickel, molybdenum or other metals. It's the chromium that puts the "stainless" into stainless steel, naturally combining with atmospheric oxygen and forming a transparent, passive film of chromium oxide that shields the metal from further oxidation. This layer actually regenerates itself if scratched or abraded.

Take a quick dip into the stainless pool and you'll find many alloys including, 301, 302, 308, 309, 321, 408, 409, 416, 430, 440, 630. I use predominantly the 300 series. The two most common and readily available 300 alloys are:

- 304, a go-to stainless used in die striking, cutlery, kitchenware, automotive parts, and fasteners.

- 316, sometimes more costly but with a higher corrosion resistance (thanks to molybdenum). It's the choice for surgical instruments, medical equipment, food preparation and harsh environments.

Brooch back basics: 20-gauge hard, springy 304 pinstem. Catch on the left, hinge on the right. The pinstem is bent to add interest to the back.

I first began using stainless years ago when I needed something strong and springy for the pin stems on my brooches. The 304 wire was so hard that it notched most side cutters or nippers, could not be cut with a jeweler's saw and ruined steel files. I quickly turned to abrasive separating discs mounted in my flexible shaft machine to cut and shape it, and sanding discs and rubberized abrasive wheels to refine it. I still use that springy 304 wire for my brooches and even ear wires.

Working with that hard wire led me to wrongly assume that all stainless steel was hard. As noted, most stainless is actually soft until worked. Some jewelers even make burnishers from the soft 304 used in inexpensive forks since it is less likely to harm a stone. But softness is relative and soft stainless is much stiffer than soft sterling. And here's the thing: hard or soft, stainless is tough. After a few bends or hammer blows stainless becomes stiff and stubborn. Stainless that hasn't been work or factory-hardened is easier to process than that spring-hard pin wire, but sanding, filing, forging and finishing stainless requires more effort than with other common jewelry metals. You have to over-bend because it wants to bounce back. But while this can make stainless more challenging during the making, that quality becomes an asset after the piece is made. I wear a fabricated stainless ring with a textured surface that I ground in with an abrasive wheel. I wear it every day. That texture looks as fresh as the day it came off the bench four years ago. In sterling it would have been gone in a month of daily wear.

That initial foray into stainless led me to think about the metal as a jewelry material in and of itself. While refilling my oxygen tank at the welding supplier I noticed a rack of stainless welding rod, various alloys and gauges. I bought a package of 16-gauge /1.3 mm rod. This rod was 316 and like all the rod in that rack was sold as TIG welding filler material. Rather than employing the rod as it was intended, I used it, along with the thinner pin wire, as a structural material. This softer 16-gauge could be hammered or rolled to flatten and widen, or add texture. With low expectations and very little plan I began building two brooches, one curvilinear and one more geometric.

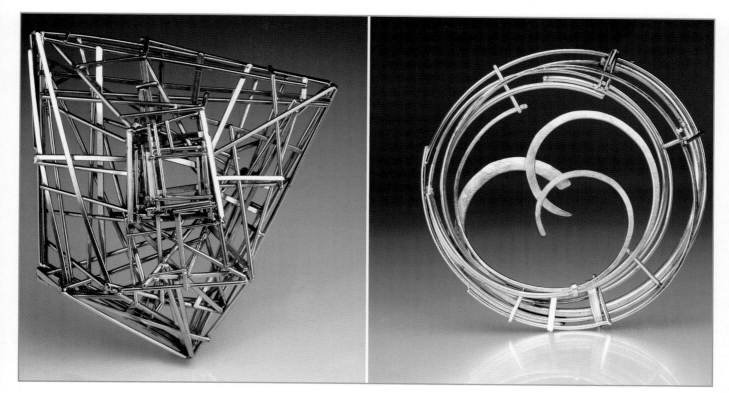

Brooches: Macle, left. Rosette, right. 3-inch (7.6 cm) width. Forged, rolled and fabricated from 304, 316, 308 & 309. I'm choosing wire less for alloy than for gauge.

I soon built more brooches, rings, neckpieces, cuffs and bangles using that original 16-gauge rod along with thicker material from the welding supplier. More interested in gauge than the alloy, I grabbed 316, 308 and 309 rod and mixed it with the 304 pin wire I had on hand (they don't make a 304 welding rod). I'm still fabricating with these rods and wires (it all comes in 36-inch (91.4 cm) straight lengths) along with 304 sheet which, while factory annealed, is still surprisingly tough. For my jewelry, mixing stainless alloys hasn't posed a structural or aesthetic problem. A professional welder or fabricator would absolutely not be so cavalier.

Which brings me to this **DISCLAIMER**.

I've been a jeweler and metalsmith for over 40 years and while I'm absolutely confident talking about gold, silver, brass, bronze and steel, my experience with stainless is newer. I am not a metallurgist, professional welder or stainless fabricator.

So, let's talk about working with the 300 series.

Annealing

Stainless gets hard pretty quickly but most alloys can be annealed using the torches in our studio. I heat the area to be annealed to a high red of 1700°F (927°C) to 1900°F (1038°C)—stainless spot heats well—and then immediately quench in water. Coating with a good jeweler's paste flux can help mitigate the nasty and tenacious black oxide that will form from heating. This can be chemically or mechanically removed. I most often grind or sand it off since it is in smaller areas. Annealing thinner wires can leave them too soft and, unless we work harden them again, they lose one of the properties that I like most about stainless.

Pickling

The 300 series stainless steels can go into standard sodium bisulfate jewelry pickles like Sparex® or pHDown®. In fact, soft 304 wire, usually sold in coils, makes a great **binding wire** since it's hard to melt, rarely solders to the work and can be dropped straight into the pickle. It's inexpensive and can be readily cut with nippers. I even use stainless hooks to hang work in my pickle pot. The exception would be some of the 400 series, often found in hobby stores, which is more magnetic and may dissolve in sodium bisulfate. With the the 300 series of stainless I've found that warm, fresh sodium bisulfate pickle will remove most of the oxides as will a fresh, warm, concentrated solution of citric acid pickle.

Rolling and Forging

Please note: I NEVER roll that hard stainless pin wire through my rolling mill. That being said—this may be blasphemy—I routinely put my other stainless welding rod and sheet goods through my mill to flatten, widen or step-roll (after I know that it is soft enough by bending or hammering it). Step-rolling is how I've learned to speed up the process of forging, or drawing, a taper in gold, silver, bronze, brass—and stainless— rod stock. While not truly forging, rolling the stock down in sequentially thinner steps develops a rough taper quickly that can then be refined by forging with a hammer.

Reality check: Less expensive rolling mills may be too soft for harder stainless since all rolls aren't hardened to the same degree. Always use caution when introducing work hardened stainless into the rolls. Never roll stainless that has a hard, heat-induced oxide.

Drilling

I use high-speed steel (HSS) drill bits that are standard issue at my bench. Keeping them lubricated with wax, bur and saw lubricant, etc. and using a slow to medium speed eases the drilling and prolongs the life of the bit. Whenever drilling into metal, I use a small ball bur rather than a centerpunch to make a pilot mark. I have more control with the bur and when drilling through rod, tube or anything hollow the centerpunch simply doesn't work. In stainless, a bur has the added advantage of grinding through harder oxides that would dull a bit quickly (the bur doesn't seem to dull as quickly).

Cutting

Sawing even factory-annealed stainless with a jeweler's saw can be slow and blades dull quickly. I cut most stainless sheet (I buy it annealed) with my bench mounted shears, up to 14-gauge, depending on the shear. Though stiffer than nonferrous metals, it shears well. Some hand-held nippers, side cutters and electrician's pliers will work on thicker wire like welding rod as will specialty cutting pliers that are made for harder materials. I usually bend or lightly hammer the metal to see how hard it is. If it bends well, I bring it to the shear. When in doubt, test it out.

Filing and Grinding

My **flexible shaft machine** is a go-to in my studio and working with stainless is no exception. My usual inclination is to grab a bur rather than a file. Large round, cylinder and even setting burs (I use the side) really move the stainless. But stainless can dull burs. Use lubrication and a slower speed.

Sanding and Refining

On larger pieces of wire or sheet I may sand by hand. I'm most likely to rely on my flex shaft with smaller or more intricate elements. In my studio, I've found the best refining tools are Snap-On® style sanding discs (I use 150 and 220-grit) and mounted sanding drums. Grit impregnated rubberized abrasive wheels and points (like Cratex® or AdvantEdge®) can be shaped as needed and can really speed things up bringing me quickly from 220 to pre-polish. I use medium, fine and extra fine grit.

From my arsenal of flexible shaft abrasives: separating discs on the left, Snap-On® discs on the right. Note the special Snap-On® mandrel.

Finishing

If I really need a fine finish, especially on larger areas, I will follow progressive sanding steps more religiously. Like platinum, stainless doesn't give up its sanding lines and scratches easily (there's that toughness again). It's best to carefully complete each course of sanding or buffing before moving to the next. Moving to finer sanding discs and 400 to 600-grit sandpaper will give a quality finish, followed by aggressive buffing/cutting compounds like Brown Tripoli, Bobbing and Graystar which will nicely smooth things out. (I got in the habit early of using whatever I had on hand, rather than stainless-specific compounds.) For a final finish, red rouge works, although a colleague turned me on to white rouge, sometimes used for platinum, which works really well on stainless.

Creating Color

Stainless can be blackened chemically or with heat. A heat-blackened area may be more prone to rust since the transparent chromium oxide layer is altered. Chemical blackening works, although those solutions can be a little spendy. Stainless steel objects can also be painted or powder coated. While relatively simple, powder coating requires a few pieces of equipment, but the cost is low and many jewelers and metalsmiths powder coat in their studio. Because of its strength, delicate structures can be built and then colored. Whether blackening or powder coating, coloring is usually the last step.

Welded stainless with red powder-coat.

Joining Stainless Steel

So, by now I'm sure you've been thinking "*How do I join stainless steel? Do I need mad-scientist level laboratory gadgets to work with it?*" Well, no—and yes(ish). This is where things can get a little complicated.

Cold Connecting

Like most of our jewelry metals and materials, stainless can be joined without heat. Riveting, lashing, twisting (annealed metal) are but a few methods. But what about using heat?

Soldering

Stainless can be silver and gold soldered (brazed) to itself or most other jewelry metals, although that will leave it annealed. As with annealing, I use a good paste flux to shield the area. At soldering temperatures that nasty black oxide (mentioned before) can form if the flux burns through. THE SOLDER WILL NOT FLOW ON THAT SURFACE. Period. You have to stop, remove the flux and the oxide and begin again. Stainless is more like gold than silver in that it does not conduct heat very well. So you can concentrate on a specific (well fluxed) area like where a stainless ear wire joins an earring. Once soldered that area will become annealed, but one or two twists will harden it nicely. I use oxy propane for all my torches but acetylene/atmospheric air (Goss, Smith, Prestolite) would work fine if the tip is small enough.

In truth, I really don't solder stainless much. I mostly weld it, meaning that I fuse or melt two elements where they meet. If I need to fill or build up an area, I use the same material, so no additional alloy is added.

Whelk earrings. Rolled, forged and fabricated sterling with 304 stainless wires. The wires are carefully soldered to the sterling.

Welding

In 2013 I invested in a Pulse Arc Welder. Pulse arc welding is a mini version of TIG (Tungsten Inert Gas), although it differs in that the welding heat is delivered in bursts (pulses) rather than continuously. Work is held in the hand during welding and viewed through a binocular microscope which auto-darkens as the weld is initiated, protecting your eyes. These welders are similar to laser welders in that very precise welds can be made in relatively heat-intolerant scenarios which is why work can be held in the hand. But laser welders use a focused beam of light to melt and weld whereas pulse arc welders create an arc of electricity to do the same. There are advantages to both technologies although pulse arc welders are a fraction of the cost of their light-emitting cousins. Pulse arc welders—there are two major brands with a variety of models—were designed for jewelers, die makers and dental techs. At the time of this writing a top-of-the-line pulse arc welder is well under $9000.00 US. (My first welder was a more basic and much less expensive model that did everything that I asked of it.)

Orion Pulse Arc Welder. Note the microscope eyepieces. The probe is at the bottom.

A Note about Safety:

- Sanding and grinding stainless should be done with proper ventilation. Ditto soldering and especially welding. Ideally a mask should also be worn.

- Welding stainless should most definitely involve ventilation.

- While the welding electrode can certainly become hot, it's the electrical arc between the tip and the point on the work you are welding that does the melting (hence pulse arc welding). In my experience, at higher welding power it's the work itself, rather than the electrode, that can become hot. (This also depends on the conductivity of the metal: sterling conducts heat quickly while gold and stainless take a while.) Wearing leather gloves or finger cots is always a good idea.

The sticker price intimidated me but I understood that this technology would open doors. With sterling, gold and bronze it allows me to tack pieces prior to soldering, speeding things up by mitigating warping and eliminating elaborate jigging. And I can build by adding metal. Drilled a hole in the wrong place on a bronze piece? Weld it shut with new bronze. Want to add some sterling to a casting? Weld away! No solder, no differing metals, no seam. Sweet!

Back to stainless: These machines seem to be made for it. In fact, stainless steel was one of those doors that I knew this technology would open. I'll say it again, work is held in the hands during welding. I have my fingers very close to the welding electrode which is melting the stainless at temperatures upwards of 2500°F (1371°C) . The metal might get warm but if I'm careful, it doesn't get hot. As with soldering I am able to weld other metals to stainless. Yellow and rose gold work very well for this while sterling makes a more brittle weld.

Pros and Cons

So, let's sum things up by looking at the reality of working with stainless.

We've looked at the good: strength and durability, low cost of materials, relatively available, pretty much tarnish free and with the proper equipment, suitable for the small studio. A piece made with stainless can really make a statement.

Then there's the not-so-great stuff:

1. Stainless can be tough, hard and stubborn.

2. Joining with heat:

    Stainless steel can be a bit tricky to torch solder. To weld it you need a welding machine such as a Laser or Pulse Arc Welder (standard MIG or TIG welders are not designed for jewelry or small-scale applications). All are readily available for the small studio but can be relatively costly.

The pulse arc welding learning curve can be quite steep and intimidating. But the only way to conquer the curve is to start climbing. A little knowledge becomes a lot of knowledge quickly. **Note**: while laser welders work great on stainless, pulse arc welders work wonderfully and are much less expensive and bulky.

3. There's that heavy black oxide, which can be quite hard, that develops from heating.

4. The native stainless color palette is limited to grays and silvers.

    I rely on juxtaposing texture, reflectivity, and structural density to give depth and character to my stainless work.

5. While a lovely surface can be produced with hammers, burs and abrasives, I haven't found a way to produce many of the torch-generated textures that characterize much of my work.

Explorations

I'm discovering new types of heat-produced surfaces, including recent experiments fusing sterling to 304 with my torch as well as with my welder to create a nodular texture, and I'm exploring other types of heat-produced surfaces. I've begun adding color by powder coating. I've been pulse arc welding gold to stainless for a while with excellent results and I'm slowly combining stainless with the materials, aesthetic, and sensibility of my other work.

And I'm not alone in these explorations. Many artists are using stainless steel as a sculptural material or, acknowledging the common perception of stainless as an industrial material, pairing it with traditional jewelry techniques like granulation or engraving and even **Damascus steel**. Stainless can be a challenging material but it's well worth the effort. As technology improves and becomes even more accessible the stainless frontier will be pushed into exciting new territory. Artists and makers will follow this frontier. There's a lot more to explore.

4. ETCHING LOW CARBON STEEL

ETCHING IS A VALUABLE SURFACE treatment for steel jewelry that enables you to add dimension, which increases visual appeal and provides a backdrop for embellishments such as stones, fused metals and Keum Boo. Nearly all metals can be etched, but the materials and processes differ depending on the metal. Etching involves many variables, so the best way to learn is to experiment and try different approaches to determine what works best for you.

Etching Process

Regardless of the etching approach used, all etching processes have two things in common, a **resist** and an **etchant**.

- **Resist**. The resist is the material that is applied to the metal surface to protect it from the etchant. The resist blocks the action of the etchant as it dissolves metal particles in the exposed areas. Wherever the resist is *not* applied, etching will occur and the metal will be recessed. The resist is one of the most critical aspects of etching. If the resist doesn't hold up and begins to disintegrate during the etching process, the result will be unsatisfactory.

- **Etchant**. The etchant, also referred to as the **mordant** or, in the case of **electro-etching**, as the **electrolyte**, is the chemical solution that causes the metal to etch. The etching process occurs when the etchant eats away (dissolves) the unprotected metal surface to produce a recessed area or depression.

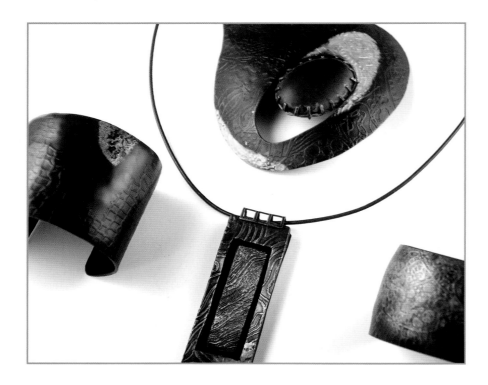

Etching is an important technique used to add dimension and increase the visual appeal of steel jewelry.

The following diagram shows a cross section of the metal illustrating how the etching process works:

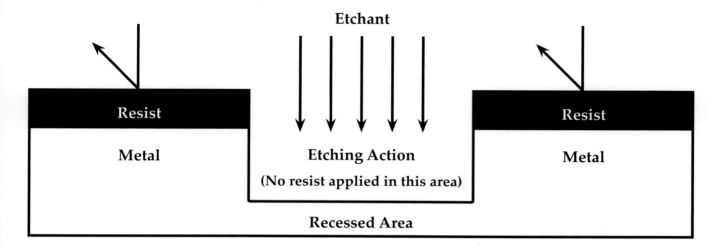

Step 1—Prepare the Metal for Etching

The steel must be free of any rust, dirt or oil that might interfere with the resist or the action of the etchant. Scrub the metal thoroughly with pumice cleaner and a brass brush until water sheets off. Rub the surface with 400-grit sandpaper or a mesh scrub pad to give the surface a slightly rough surface, which helps the resist adhere. As a final step, use a paper towel or clean cloth to wipe the metal with denatured or isopropyl alcohol. Do not use acetone as it leaves a residue that can interfere with the ability of the resist to adhere.

Step 2—Apply the Resist

I have used three types of resists successfully: oil paint, laser printed transfer and adhesive-backed stencil.

Oil Paint Resist. Oil paint is a sturdy resist that is available in many forms, including oil paint pens, tubes, cans and spray paint. Be sure to use oil paint because acrylic paint is likely to break down during the etching process. Oil paint gives you the option of drawing or painting your etching designs freehand on the metal surface. Simple patterns and designs produce the best etches, so you do not need to be a skilled illustrator. You can sketch your design out first on the metal using a pencil and then retrace your sketch with oil paint.

Oil paint pens are a great option because they give you control over drawing designs. Be sure to select a pen that will leave a clean, sharp line on the metal and which holds up to the etching solution.

Resist created using an oil paint pen.

Any type of oil-based paint will work—even nail polish. If you use spray paint, it's a good idea to do so outdoors and hold the spray can an arm-length away from the metal to get a spattered effect. After applying oil paint, allow it to air dry completely for an hour or, ideally, overnight. To speed the drying, use a heat gun or hair dryer.

If you are not satisfied with your design or make a mistake, simply use paint thinner or turpentine to remove the paint, re-wipe with alcohol and reapply.

Resist created using fingernail polish.

Resist created using spray oil paint.

Laser Printed Transfer Resist. A design printed using a laser printer works well as a resist although it is not as durable as oil paint. The process involves printing an illustration, graphic design or high-contrast photograph and transferring the printed design to the metal. The printer must be a laser printer; an inkjet printer will not work. Laser printers use a toner powder, essentially powdered plastic, that is deposited on the paper.

Examples of laser printed images appropriate for transfer to metal.

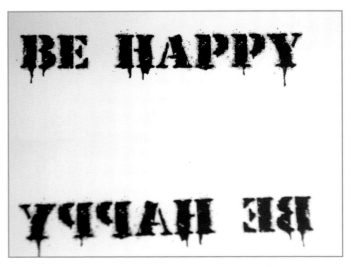

Laser printed image of text that has been reversed so that it will transfer correctly to the metal.

Most brands of laser printers will work, but some people have reported that occasionally certain later model printers do not work well because the formula for the toner requires a higher heat to soften.

Use a glossy-coated lighter weight paper for printing the design. Heavy photography paper is not recommended because it is more difficult to remove from the metal after transferring the laser printed resist. Glossy magazine paper will also work.

Just print your design right over the printed surface of the paper. Other papers or films that will work include toner transfer paper, blue transfer film and circuit board thermal transfer paper; however, I have had good results using glossy printer paper.

Laser printed transfer that has been converted to line art.

Here are the steps for creating and transferring a laser printed design:

- **Choose and print your design**. Choose line art or a design with high contrast. Avoid images with fine lines and subtle shading because these are likely to break up in the etching solution. The image will be transferred in reverse so if you're etching a design that has a specific direction, for example text, convert to a reversed image using a graphic program. A high contrast photo will also work but you will need to convert it to black and white, reverse it and then convert it to line art in a graphic program such as Adobe Photoshop®. If necessary, resize your image to ensure that it fits the piece of metal that you want to etch.

  Set your printer to black and white at the highest density to obtain the darkest image. If you are printing on toner transfer paper, transfer film, or circuit board paper, be sure to follow the instructions for printing on the proper side, usually the matte side. After you have printed the image, cut the paper to fit the piece of metal that you intend to etch. Place your printed image face down on clean metal.

This image will work well as a transfer because it has bold sharp lines without a lot of shading.

This image is unlikely to transfer well because it has fine lines and a lot of shading.

- **Transfer the design to the metal**. Use a heat source, such as an electric hotplate or griddle, to soften the toner and transfer it to the surface of the metal. Set the temperature control to medium high or 300° to 350°F (150° to 175°C). Carefully place the metal/paper sandwich on the heat source, metal side on the bottom without letting the paper shift. Allow it to warm for three to five minutes. Using two burnishers or the backs of two spoons, hold the paper steady with one hand while burnishing it with the other across the entire surface. If the paper begins to scorch, reduce the heat. Continue to burnish the paper. You may want to place another piece of metal on top of the paper to avoid loss of heat from the surface. After burnishing the paper for a few moments, carefully lift a corner to check whether the toner has begun to transfer. If the toner still has broken spots, carefully replace the edge of the paper and continue to burnish for another few minutes. Keep checking. Be careful not to let it go too long or the toner will melt and become splotchy.

A tee shirt press or laminator can also be used as a heat source to transfer laser printed designs. Be sure to follow the press or laminator instructions. You'll need to run the metal/paper sandwich multiple times to achieve a good transfer of the toner.

Place the transfer face down on the metal.

Burnish the paper thoroughly until the toner has transferred to the metal.

Carefully lift a corner of the paper to check the progress of the transfer.

- **Remove the paper and inspect**. Once the toner is transferred, remove the metal from the heat source, allow it to cool for a few seconds and slowly and carefully peel the paper back from the surface. If the paper sticks, you can soak it in warm water until the paper softens and rub it off with your fingers.

The laser toner has been successfully transferred to the metal.

Adhesive-Backed Stencil Resist. Adhesive-backed vinyl stencils provide a simple and very effective resist. They are available from arts and crafts stores and online. Do not use silk screening stencils as these have a fine mesh that will interfere with the etching action. Measure and trim the stencil to fit the piece of metal you are etching. Allow about a one-fourth-inch overlap around the edges. Remove the backing and carefully stick the stencil to the cleaned metal, making sure that it is placed exactly where you want it before pressing it firmly into place. Rub the stencil down using a burnisher or metal spoon to remove all the air bubbles. Note that this will give you what is called an intaglio (incised) etch, meaning that the open parts of the stencil will be etched and the background will be raised. If you want a relief etch where the open parts will be raised, daub oil paint onto the open areas of the stencil, allow the paint to dry and peel the stencil off.

Adhesive-backed stencils are available in many designs.

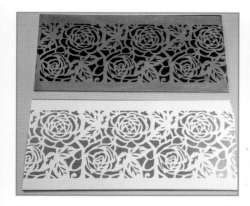

The stencil creates an intaglio etch with the design recessed. To create a relief etch, with a raised design, use oil paint to fill in the open areas of the stencil, allow to dry and peel off the stencil.

Use a burnisher to firmly bond the stencil to the metal.

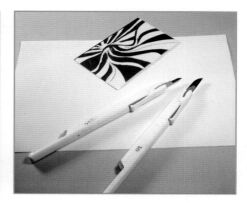

You can purchase uncut adhesive-backed vinyl sheets and cut your own custom stencils using a craft knife.

Adhesive-backed stencils can be reused by spraying the back with a repositionable spray adhesive. Also, uncut sheets of adhesive-backed vinyl sheets are available with which you can cut your own custom stencil design using a craft knife or electric stencil cutting pen.

Vinyl cutting machines allow you to create custom vinyl stencils that can be used as resists for etching. Each cutter is used in combination with a computer program designed for it. There is a learning curve for using a cutter, but many tutorials are available on YouTube.

Step 3—Mix the Etchant

Here I will cover the three etchants that I recommend for low carbon steel: copper sulfate/salt solution, copper nitrate solution, and salt/citric acid solution. These chemicals are less toxic and safer than traditional etching acids used in the past, such as hydrochloric acid. However, when the chemicals are diluted in water they produce acids, which can cause eye, lung and skin irritation. When mixing and using etching chemicals, wear protective gloves and safety glasses. Work in a well-ventilated area and avoid breathing the fumes.

It's also a good idea to review the safety specifications for each chemical. Be sure to protect your clothing because etching solutions will stain fabrics.

 Safety alert: When etching chemicals are added to water, they form mild acids, which can be caustic and harmful if inhaled. Be sure to wear protective gloves, safety glasses and breathing protection.

Glass and plastic straight-sided containers are useful for the etching solution.

I use tap water to mix etchants, but if your tap water has a high mineral content or if you are uncertain, you should use distilled water. It is helpful to use warm water which dissolves the chemicals more quickly. Use a non-reactive container (plastic or glass) that is large enough to accommodate your work. I prefer a straight-sided lidded plastic food storage container because it can also store etching solution between uses.

Safety alert: When mixing the etching solution, slowly add the chemicals to the water to avoid splashing and prevent any heat production that can be caused by adding liquids to acidic chemicals.

Slowly add the chemicals to the water to avoid splashing and to prevent any heat production that can be caused by adding liquids to acidic chemicals. Use a non-reactive glass or plastic stick or spoon to stir the solution until most of the chemicals are dissolved. Don't worry if some of the chemicals remain undissolved. That simply means that the solution is fully saturated.

Copper sulfate is a bright blue-green powder or crystalline chemical that is often sold in hardware stores and plant nurseries as a root killer.

Copper Sulfate and Salt Solution. Copper sulfate (cupric sulphate) is a chemical that is used primarily for agricultural purposes as a pesticide, germicide, feed additive, and soil additive. It is available in two forms: the anhydrous form ($CuSO_4$) and copper sulfate pentahydrate ($CuSO_4 \cdot 5H_2O$), the hydrated form that has water added. Either form will work for the etchant. Copper sulfate is often sold in hardware stores or plant nurseries and under various brand names as a root killer. Check the label to ensure that the primary ingredient is cupric sulfate pentahydrate with no more than trace amounts of other chemicals. For the salt (sodium chloride, NaCl), use non-iodized salt without any added ingredients such as anti-caking agents.

To each quart of water (approximately one liter) add:

½-cup (120-milliliters) of copper sulfate.
½-cup (120-milliliters) of non-iodized salt.
Optional 1 to 2 tablespoons (15 to 30-milliliters) of citric acid.

Copper Nitrate Solution. Cupric nitrate, $Cu(NO_3)_2$, is a blue-green crystalline chemical available from chemical supply shops. It is an oxidizer and is used as a fixant in dying textiles and creating various finishes on metals.

Copper nitrate is a blue-green crystal that can be purchased from chemical suppliers.

> **To each quart of water (approximately one liter) add:**
>
> ¾-cup (180-milliliters) copper nitrate.
> Optional 1 to 2 tablespoons (15 to 30-milliliters) of citric acid.

Salt and Citric Acid Solution. Non-iodized salt, NaCl, is readily available in grocery stores and is often sold as kosher salt. When added to water it is an effective solution for electro-etching. It will not work without electricity. The electro-etching process is described later in this section.

> **To each quart of water (approximately one liter) add:**
>
> 1 to 1-¼ cup (240 to 300-milliliters) of salt.
> Optional 1 to 2 tablespoons (15 to 30-milliliters) citric acid.

Use non-iodized salt without any added ingredients such as anti-caking agents. Add salt to hot water and keep stirring until the salt no longer dissolves, indicating that the solution is fully saturated.

Step 4—Etch the Metal

Once the solution is mixed, choose the etching method you want to use—either chemical or electro-etching. All the solutions described will work with electro-etching. However, the salt/citric acid solution will only work with the electro-etching method. Both etching methods can produce outstanding results. However, I generally prefer electro-etching because it is more controllable and produces better results for fine lines and delicate patterns.

Your goal is to create a sharply etched pattern without streaks or breaks. A clean etch is also free of undercutting, which occurs when the etchant eats under the edges of the resist causing a ragged edge. The following diagram illustrates the difference between a clean etch and one that has been undercut. In the first one, the sidewalls of the resist are straight; in the second, the sidewalls have been eaten away below the resist resulting in a more ragged etch.

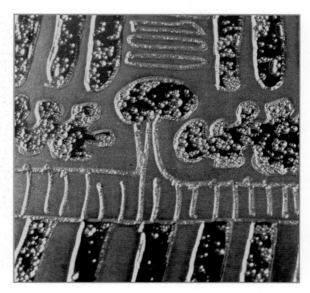

An example of an unsatisfactory etch that is broken and undercut.

Clean

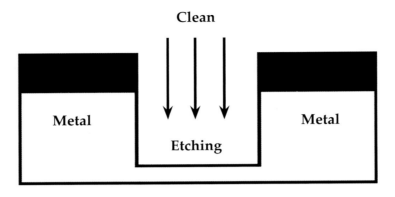

Undercut

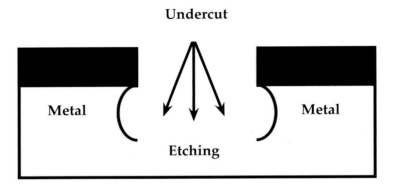

You'll need the following materials for the chemical etching process:

1. **Container with etching solution** (copper sulfate/salt or copper nitrate solution).
2. **Warming device** such as a hot plate, electric griddle, coffee cup warmer (not an immersion warmer) or a hot pad to speed the etching process.
3. **Aquarium pump and bubbler** to avoid streaks and uneven etching.
4. **Wooden dowel**, or metal rod long enough to be placed across the mouth of the container.
5. **Duct tape** to protect the back of the metal from etching.
6. **Paint brush** to remove residue that collects on the surface of the metal.

Chemical Etching Process. Cover the back of the metal piece that you want to etch with duct tape. You can also cover the edges of the metal if you wish, but I have not found this necessary as the etchant does not roughen the edges significantly. Place the dowel or rod across the top of the container. Then secure a piece of duct tape from the back of the piece up to the dowel and hang the metal from the dowel down into the solution. Make sure that the piece is fully submerged in the solution.

Warming the solution slightly with a hot plate, electric griddle, coffee cup warmer or hot pad helps make it more chemically active and speeds the etching process. Place a piece of aluminum foil or silicone baking pad on the warming device to protect it from drips. Using an aquarium bubbler helps keep the solution in circulation and avoids streaks or bubbles that might be caused by residue settling on the metal. Place the aquarium bubbler inside the container so that it rests on the bottom. If necessary, use a piece of duct tape at the top of the container to hold the bubbler in place.

Turn on the warming device and bubbler and start timing the etching process. After about 15 minutes, lift the metal piece from the solution and brush off any residue. Wearing rubber gloves, rub your finger across the surface to check the depth of the etch in the metal's surface. The goal is to feel a defined ridge in the surface. It is difficult to measure, but use your fingernail and aim for about a millimeter of depth. If the etch is not yet deep enough, re-submerge the piece and continue to check it every 15 minutes until the etched pattern is well defined, crisp and clear. You can leave the metal in the solution until the etch is as deep as you wish, but if you see that the resist is starting to break up or deteriorate, it is time to remove the metal from the solution.

Safety alert: Protect your warming device from liquids by placing aluminum foil over it.

Set-up for chemical etching with a hotplate to warm the solution and an aquarium bubbler to keep the solution circulating.

Remove the piece every 15 minutes to check the etching process. Use a brush to remove residue.

Electro-etching Process.

You'll need the following materials for the electro-etching process:

1. **Container with etching solution**.
2. **Wooden dowel** or metal rod long enough to be placed across the mouth of the container.
3. **Duct tape** to protect the back of the metal from being etched.
4. **Paint brush** to remove residue that collects on the surface of the metal.
5. **Small strip of conductive metal** (copper or steel), one-half-inch to one-inch (12 to 25-millimeters) wide by approximately 4 to 6-inches (100 to 150-millimeters) long.
6. **Sheet of conductive metal** (copper or steel) larger than the piece you are etching which extends slightly above the mouth of the container.
7. **Source of electricity**, for example:
   - Two D batteries placed in a plastic battery holder with attached leads. Attach alligator clips to the leads.
   - Rectifier (variable power supply). This is an electrical device that converts alternating current from your home electrical outlets to direct current, which flows in one direction and is what we use for etching.

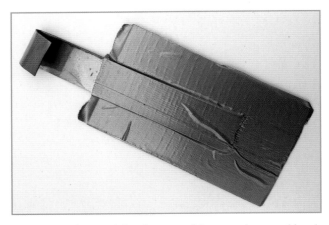

To prepare the metal for electro-etching, attach a metal hook to the back of the piece and tape securely with duct tape, covering the entire back. Use the hook to suspend the piece from the dowel or metal rod resting across the top of the container.

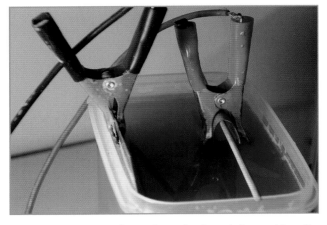

Attach the negative clip to the cathode and the positive clip to the anode.

Two D batteries can be used to provide the electricity for the electro-etching process.

Form a hook at one end of the small metal strip and use duct tape to firmly attach the other end to the back of your metal piece, making sure both the small strip of metal and your piece are in contact without any tape in between. Cover the entire back of your piece with duct tape to avoid etching it. You can also cover the edges of the metal if you wish, but I have not found this necessary as the etchant does not roughen the edges significantly. Use the hook to suspend your piece from the dowel or rod, completely submerging your piece in the solution.

Place the larger metal sheet inside the etching container and lean it against the side. Attach the negative alligator clip (black wire) to the sheet making sure the clip is firmly in contact with the metal and is not submerged. This sheet will serve as the cathode, or negatively charged electrode. The piece that is being etched should be parallel and approximately 1 to 2-inches (12 to 25-millimeters) away from the cathode. Attach the positive alligator clip (red wire) to the metal hook that is attached to your piece, which will serve as the positively charged electrode).

If you are using a rectifier, adjust the voltage until the amps are between 1.5 to 2.0. You may need to fine tune the setting by adjusting the amperage knob. Each power supply operates slightly differently and you should follow the instructions to adjust the power input and output properly.

The etching solution, referred to as the electrolyte, completes the electrical circuit between the cathode and anode, and the exposed metal of the anode begins to dissolve into the electrolyte solution. Particles of metal will move along with the current. If you're using a salt/citric acid solution, you'll see small bubbles form and move from the anode to the cathode. This will be a sign that etching is occurring.

After 10 to 15 minutes lift the piece that you are etching from the solution, leaving the hook and clip attached, and use the brush to wipe off any residue. Rub your gloved finger across the surface to check the etching process. Re-submerge the piece and continue to check it every 10 to 15 minutes. If you are using a rectifier, you'll notice that the amps will increase after you clean the surface and then they will gradually drop. Occasionally pull the cathode from the solution and brush residue off the surface.

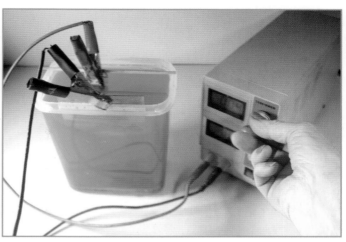

If you are using a power supply (also referred to as a rectifier) follow the instructions to adjust the settings so that the output reads between 1.5 and 2.0 amps.

Check the etching process every 10 to 15 minutes. If using a rectifier, you may need to adjust the settings to maintain the proper amperage.

Completing the Process. The speed of the etching process depends on many factors including the freshness and saturation of the solution, the size of the cathode and the distance between the cathode and anode. The etching process can take anywhere from 15 minutes to an hour or even more with larger pieces.

After you are satisfied with the depth of the etch, remove the piece from the solution. If you're using electro-etching, turn off the power source and remove the clips from the cathode and anode. Clean the metal hook, alligator clips and cathode and dry them thoroughly to prevent corrosion. Rinse your piece and remove the resist. Peel off any plastic stencil or vinyl resist. Oil paint, toner transfer and residue from stencils or vinyl can usually be scrubbed off with a brass or steel brush and pumice cleaner. Any remaining resist can be removed using paint thinner or turpentine, followed by alcohol.

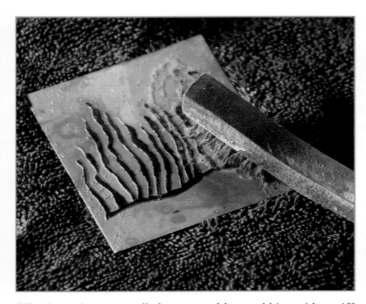

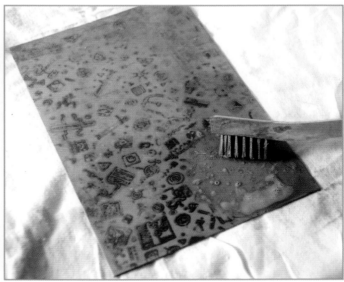

Oil paint resist can usually be removed by scrubbing with a stiff brass brush and pumice cleanser. Any remaining oil paint can be removed using turpentine.

Toner transfer resist can be removed by scrubbing with a stiff brass brush and pumice cleanser.

Remove the stencil and wipe the metal with alcohol or acetone to remove any adhesive residue.

When the etching solution is fresh it is more aggressive and it will continue to work over a period before the etching action declines. The length of time that the solution remains potent depends on the size of the pieces you are etching and the frequency of use. Between uses store the solution in a sealed container away from direct sunlight.

As the solution builds up a heavy deposit of sediment, you can filter it using coffee filters or fabric from old tee-shirts. As solutions start losing their potency, you can revive them a bit by adding a small amount of chemicals.

Disposing of the Solution. Spent etching solutions should be disposed of properly at a chemical waste facility. Pouring them down the drain or dumping them outside is environmentally irresponsible because the chemicals can be harmful to wildlife. I keep a big plastic bucket to collect spent solutions and cover it with plastic until it is full enough to warrant a trip to the disposal center.

Troubleshooting the Etching Process

- **Oil paint resist breaks up or erodes during the etching process**. The problem could be with either the resist or the etching process. Be sure that you are using oil paint (not acrylic) and that it is completely dry. If the etching solution is fresh, it will be more aggressive and can eat through the oil paint resist more quickly. In this case, check the progress more frequently and remove the piece as soon as you notice any breaks in the resist. Finally, if you are electro-etching using a rectifier, be sure that your amperage does not exceed 2.0.

- **Laser printed resist does not transfer to the metal**. Be sure that you are using a laser printer as inkjet printers will not work for this process. Also, rarely, some later model printers use a different toner formulation that will not work for transfers. If your image has fine lines or shading, it will probably not transfer well. Finally, be sure that you are using sufficient heat to soften the toner so that it transfers effectively.

- **Etched areas are rough and streaky**. With chemical etching, this problem can likely be corrected by using an aquarium bubbler to keep the solution in circulation around the metal thus preventing residue from building and blocking the etching action. With either type of etching process, this result can be caused by neglecting to clean residue off the metal at appropriate intervals.

- **The metal is not etching at all or the etching process is extremely slow**. If your etching solution has been used a number of times, it may have lost its potency and it is time to mix a fresh solution. If you are electro-etching, check to ensure that the alligator clips are making a solid connection with the metal to complete the electric circuit. It is common for the clips to corrode with use, requiring cleaning and filing them down to ensure a solid connection. Also check the wires to ensure that none of the connections are broken. If you are using batteries, it may be time to replace them. If you are using a rectifier, check the settings to ensure that the amperage is set at 1.5 to 2.0.

5. FUSING GOLD & OTHER METALS TO STEEL

FUSING GOLD AND OTHER NON-FERROUS metals to low carbon steel is at the heart of my work. Technically speaking, the fusing process is an atomic interaction between metals called **liquid state diffusion** which enables non-ferrous metals to be melted and fused to steel. The process involves heating the steel and a non-ferrous metal together until the latter melts and its atoms intersperse with those of the steel. Remember, mild steel has a relatively high melting temperature, roughly 2600°F (1427°C) so you can fuse nearly all metals with a lower metal temperature to it.

Gold and its alloys are the most popular metals for fusing to steel largely because of the wide range of colors and **karat** variations possible and gold's dramatic contrast against blackened steel. Twenty-four karat gold, with its rich yellow color and perceived value, is a beautiful choice, but there are many gold alloys that offer a huge range of attractive effects.

Creating Gold Alloys for Fusing to Steel

Metal alloys are combinations of two or more metals and sometimes non-metals. Most gold alloys are available commercially so alloying your own is not essential to the fusing process. However, alloying metals is a valuable and satisfying skill that enables metalsmiths to create the exact metal formulations needed for various applications. Different alloys have different characteristics, and the ability to alloy metals gives metal artists the flexibility to tailor the composition according to their requirements. In addition, alloying gives the artist the flexibility to create customized metal combinations as needed.

When selecting gold alloys for fusing to steel, three factors should be considered: karat, color and melting temperature.

Karat

Karat (k) is a measure of gold fineness and is determined by the percentage of fine gold (24k) in the alloy. It defines gold's quality and value. Each karat equals 1/24 of the amount of fine gold in an alloy. The higher the karat the greater the percentage of pure gold there is. "Pure" gold is not actually pure as it has a small percentage of impurities. So, for example, 24k gold is 24 parts or 100 percent gold, and 18k gold is 18 parts gold and 6 parts other metals, or in other words, 75 percent gold and 25 percent other metals. Outside of the U.S. karat is commonly spelled as "carat", which is also used as a unit of weight to measure gemstones.

In Western countries 24k gold is rarely used for jewelry because it is a relatively soft metal that damages easily. But when fusing gold and its alloys to steel, softness is not an issue because the layer of fused gold is very thin. Karat does make a difference however in how smoothly the metal diffuses across the surface of the steel. The higher the karat of the gold, the more evenly it will spread and flow. Other factors also affect the flow and spread of gold, but karat is an important one. While lower karat alloys tend to produce a less even flow, this result can be quite attractive and therefore intentional.

Color

24k gold is a beautiful buttery yellow. When other alloying metals are added, a range of colors can be produced.

For example:

- **Copper** (Cu) moves the alloy toward a rose or reddish color.
- **Silver** (Ag) moves the alloy toward a greenish color.
- **Zinc** (Zn) produces a bleached appearance.
- **Nickel** (Ni) and **Palladium** (Pd) whiten the alloy.

The color differences among gold alloys are subtle, but when they are placed side by side it is easy to distinguish them. At each karat, the color varies based on the amount of alloying metal added. A wider range of colors can be achieved as the karat is lowered.

You can see the effect of different karats in these examples of fused yellow gold.

Keep in mind that the presence of copper in any alloy will result in oxidation, which will need to be removed. Combining gold, silver and copper in different proportions can produce many colored gold alloys. These three metals can be alloyed to create yellow, red and green gold as well as subtle hues of those colors.

Each alloy has a formula that determines the karat and color. The following table shows the formulas for some of the more common gold alloys.

GOLD/COPPER/SILVER ALLOYS				
Type	Gold, wt.%	Silver, wt.%	Copper, wt.%	Hue
22K	91.6	8.4	-	Yellow
	91.6	5.5	2.8	Yellow
	91.6	3.2	5.1	Deep Yellow
	91.6	-	8.4	Pinkish Yellow
18K	75.0	25.0	-	Greenish Yellow
	75.0	16.0	9.0	Pale Yellow
	75.0	12.5	12.5	Yellow
	75.0	9.0	16.0	Pink
	75.0	4.5	20.5	Red
14K	58.5	41.5	-	Pale Green
	58.5	30.0	11.5	Yellow
	58.5	9.0	32.5	Red

Melting Temperature

24k gold melts at 1948°F (1064°C). The alloys of gold melt over a range of different temperatures, which decrease as the karat is lowered. This factor is important when combining different alloys or other metals because fusing should occur in the order of descending melting temperatures.

Casting grain, available from metal suppliers, is the most convenient and cost-effective form of metal to use for creating alloys because the grains are easier to weigh in small amounts. The "grains" are little balls of metal about 2 to 5 mm in diameter that are used by jewelers to cast one-of-a-kind jewelry items. Casting grain is available in the form of pure metals and as some pre-alloyed metals. However, if you prefer, you can use any form of metal to create alloys including sheet and wire. If you are remelting an existing alloy, be sure it does not contain any contaminants, such as solder.

Weighing Metals for Alloys

When alloying metals, you will need a digital jeweler's scale (gram scale) to weigh the various components. Battery operated or rechargeable jeweler scales are readily available from jewelry suppliers and other vendors. They vary in quality and accuracy, and I recommend that the scale you use has the capability of measuring at least to the nearest 1/10th gram (1/100th if you want greater accuracy). Although scales vary, most have the following features:

- **Automatic tare**. When you turn the scale on, the display will show a row of 8s, which is quickly replaced with a zero. This means that the scale has tared or zeroed out any weight on it. Now any object (e.g. container) placed on the scale before it is turned on will automatically have its weight tared (deducted) and you will be ready to weigh the various components of the alloy.

- **Manual tare**. While the scale is turned on if you need to tare or zero out the weight of a container or other object simply press the tare button to move the display to zero so that you are ready to weigh only the components of the alloy.

- **Mode**. Jeweler gram scales have four or five units of measure, including grams (g), ounces (oz), troy ounces (t oz. or oz t.), pennyweight (dwt.) and grain (gn). I select grams when measuring small amounts of metals for alloying and round the weight to the nearest 1/10th of a gram. If you are alloying larger quantities, you may wish to select ounces as the mode.

Units of Measure: Troy vs. Avoirdupois Weight Systems

Throughout history the system that has been used to measure precious metals has been called the troy weights system, which originated in 15th century England. The units are the grain, the pennyweight (dwt. = 24 grains), the troy ounce (oz t. = 20 dwt.) and the troy pound (12 oz t.).

The avoirdupois weight system, which is commonly used in most English-speaking countries, consists of pounds, ounces, grams and grains. A grain is of the same weight in both the avoirdupois and the troy systems, but that's where the commonalities end. For example, an ounce in the avoirdupois system is 28.35 g, but a troy ounce is slightly heavier at 31.1 g.

If you order precious metals by the pennyweight, you will need to convert the weight to grams. A pennyweight (dwt.) in the troy weights system equals 1.56 g in the avoirdupois system.

This jeweler scale is being used to weigh 4.0 grams of gold casting grains.

There are a couple of different ways to determine the weight of each component in your gold alloy. A simple way is to decide the total weight of the alloy you wish to create and then work from that amount. Estimating that amount may involve some guesswork, but keep in mind that a little bit of non-ferrous alloy goes a long way when it is being used for fusing to steel so start with a small amount. For example, let's say you want to create 10 grams of 18k pink gold alloy. The formula is 75% Au + 9% Ag + 16% Cu.* To create 10 g of 18k pink gold, here is the calculation:

*iMakeJewelry, developed by Victoria Lansford, is an invaluable web application for iPhone that provides different jewelry related calculators including one for creating alloys and one for adjusting the karat of various alloys. The calculator makes quick work of determining the appropriate proportions of metals to include in various alloys.

> **10 g x 75% = 7.5 g Au**
>
> **10 g x 9% = 0.9 g Ag**
>
> **10 g x 16% = 1.6 g Cu**
>
> **Total 10.0 g 18k pink gold alloy**

Another way to calculate the weight of the various components is to start with the amount of fine gold you have. Let's say you have 4 grams of fine gold (Au) and you want to create 18k pink gold. Here are the steps:

1. **Divide** the number of Au grams by the percentage of 24k gold in the formula to determine the total weight of the alloy. Remember to *divide* by the percentage—not multiply. This will give you the total weight of the gold alloy.

2. **Multiply** the total weight by the percentage for each alloying metal to find its weight.

Here's the math:

> **4.0 g Au divided by 0.75 = 5.3 g total weight**
>
> **5.3 g x 9% = 0.5 g Ag**
>
> **5.3 g x 16% = 0.8 g Cu**

After you have weighed the metals for your alloy, set each aside in a separate container. In this example, you will have 4 g Au, 0.5 g Ag, 0.8 g Cu. Note that the numbers have been rounded to the nearest 1/10th percent.

The Alloying Process

To alloy gold and other metals in preparation for fusing to steel, you will need the following supplies:

*   Small crucible made of fused silica or clay/silica with a handle *or* a hard charcoal block with a well that has been carved into it using a ball bur. The well should be approximately 1-inch (25 mm) in diameter and ½-inch (12.5 mm) deep.
*   Jeweler's torch that produces sufficient heat to melt metals.
*   Powdered borax.
*   Pickle pot for non-ferrous metals.

If you are using a new crucible, you must first season it to prevent cracking. To do so, use your torch to heat the crucible until it is a dull orange. Then sprinkle some borax into the bowl and direct your torch flame to the back of the bowl. The borax will act as a flux as it melts. Continue heating and the borax will begin to flow and coat the surface. Swirl it around to spread the borax and add more until the entire surface is coated and shiny. Be sure to coat the spout well with the melted borax. Maintain separate crucibles for gold and silver alloys.

> **Safety alert**: When alloying metals, wear welding glasses (#3 or #4 lenses) to protect your eyes from the orange light that is emitted from the metal.

A new crucible being seasoned with borax powder to prevent cracking.

A new charcoal block ready to use for alloying. A ball bur has been used to carve a well for melting the alloy.

Here are the steps for alloying metals:

1   **Heat the crucible or charcoal block**. Use your torch to heat the crucible or charcoal block until it is glowing a dull orange.

2   **Add the primary metal**. Add your primary metal (the largest component) to the crucible or charcoal block and place the hottest part of the flame (just beyond the blue cone) on the metal. Hold the flame steady rather than circling around the metal so that the heat will efficiently melt the metal and the flame will cover the metal, preventing absorption of oxygen.

3   **Add the other metals**. As soon as the first metal is melted, add the metal with the next highest melting temperature and continue heating until fully melted. An exception is copper. Even though its melting temperature (1983°F/1084°C) is higher than that of silver (1762°F/961°C), copper oxidizes quickly and so should be added last. Continue with the final component until all metals are melted. Keep the hottest part of the flame on the metal until it begins to lighten somewhat in color.

4   **Clear any impurities**. If impurities, referred to as **dross**, form on the surface, add a pinch of borax to clarify.

5   **Heat the alloy**. Observe the molten metal as it begins to turn lighter in color. As it nears a very bright—almost whitish color—that is your cue that the alloy's components are fully diffused, meaning the crystalline structures of all components are evenly mixed. Do not allow the metal to boil.

6   **Allow to cool**. Take your torch away from the metal and allow it to cool slightly until it becomes a dull orange.

7   **Remove the button of metal**. Wait a few more seconds and then turn the crucible or charcoal block over and tap gently to remove the small button of metal. If the metal sticks, use a solder pick to gently pry it out. Don't allow it to cool completely, or it will stick to the crucible or charcoal block. If necessary, place the alloy in the pickle to remove any oxidation.

 Safety alert: Be sure to allow the alloy to cool until it is a dull orange and is not glowing. If you remove the alloy too soon it may still be molten…a dangerous prospect!

Step 1–Heat the crucible or charcoal block until it is glowing a dull orange.

Step 2–Pour the primary metal into the charcoal block or crucible and heat until completely melted.

Step 3–Separately pour each of the other alloying metals into the charcoal block and heat until melted. Add them in the order of decreasing melting temperature, except copper, which should be added last because of its tendency to oxidize quickly.

Step 4–Clear any impurities from the surface of the molten alloy by sprinkling a small amount of borax over the surface.

Step 5–Continue heating the alloy until it is a bright, nearly white color. Keep your torch flame close to the metal to prevent oxygen from being absorbed into it.

Step 6–Allow the alloy to cool until it loses its bright color and becomes a very dull orange.

Step 7–Turn the charcoal block or crucible over and gently tap to remove the alloy. If it sticks, use your solder pick to pry it out.

Preparing Metals for Fusing to Steel

After creating your alloy you will need to prepare it for fusing to steel by rolling it into a very thin sheet in a rolling mill. Start by taping the metal button securely to a bench block or anvil using duct tape to hold it in place and then forge it flat with a heavy hammer. The purpose is to flatten the button of metal so that it can then be rolled in the rolling mill. At this point the metal will be hard and very stiff because its crystalline structure has been compressed by forging. To soften the metal, anneal it by heating it gently with a torch until it is a dull orange. This realigns the crystalline structure and makes the metal ductile. If the metal has become oxidized, pickle it and clean it, then begin rolling it out in the mill. The goal is to create a very thin strip of metal. This requires multiple rounds of rolling and annealing. Don't worry if the metal develops cracks because it is going to be cut into small pallions. Simply anneal it and continue the process until you have a thin sheet that is as thin as you can get it, which will be approximately 30-gauge (0.25 mm) in thickness. If you want to avoid cracking or splitting, you should rotate the metal 180 degrees and flip it with each pass.

Using sharp hand shears, cut the strip into very small chips or pallions approximately 3 to 4 mm using the same technique as needed for cutting sheet solder; cut a fringe and then crosscut into small pallions. Collect the pallions and store them in a small container labeled with the metal or alloy. The alloy is now ready for fusing.

Use duct tape to secure the alloy button to a bench block or anvil to prevent it from escaping during forging.

Use a heavy flat hammer to flatten the button into a pancake, thin enough to roll through the rolling mill. This step also helps remove any trapped air that can cause bubbles and cracks as the metal is rolled.

After annealing the flattened button, begin rolling it through the mill.

Whenever the metal becomes stiff and difficult to roll, anneal and pickle it.

Keep rolling and annealing until the strip of metal is as thin as your mill can achieve, usually less than 30-gauge.

Use sharp scissors to cut the metal into small pallions, approximately 3 to 4 mm.

Fusing Process

Now you're ready to fuse! The process is straightforward. The goal is to melt the non-ferrous metal across the surface of the steel before oxidation and scale can build up and interfere with the fusing action. Before beginning, be sure the steel is thoroughly cleaned using pumice cleaner, followed by using a mesh scrub pad or fine sandpaper to slightly roughen the surface. Sandblasting is also an ideal method for preparing the surface. As a final step, clean the steel with a metal degreaser or alcohol (denatured or isopropyl). As already mentioned, do not use acetone as it has an additive that leaves a residue on the metal.

The torch you use for fusing must produce sufficient heat to melt the non-ferrous metal. Dual gas torches—fuel plus oxygen—and acetylene/ambient air torches work well. Single gas torches, such as small handheld butane torches or propane torches will not produce sufficient heat for fusing. Certain kilns and forges that have a **reducing atmosphere** where the flow of oxygen is restricted may work provided they can reach the melting temperature of the metal being fused; however, I have never tested this. The fusing process is slightly different depending on the type of torch you use, as described in this section.

> **Safety alert:** When fusing metals, wear welding glasses (#3 or #4 lenses) to protect your eyes from the orange light that is emitted from the metal.

Using a Dual Gas Torch (Propane/Oxygen, Acetylene/Oxygen, Natural Gas/Oxygen)

With a fuel/oxygen torch, fusing occurs more quickly than with an acetylene/ambient air torch, but oxidation is heavier and more cleanup is required. Here are the steps when using a dual gas torch:

1 **Apply flux**. Apply flux to the front and back of the piece in the areas where the metal will be fused. Flux helps protect the metal from extreme oxidation and scale. Any paste flux can be used, but I recommend a brazing flux because it remains active longer and does a better job of protecting the steel during the fusing process. In my experience, a black brazing flux, such as Handy Flux B-1® or Harris Stay-Silv Brazing Flux®, are both effective and remain active to 1800°F (980°C). These brazing fluxes are basically white flux with boron powder added, which extends the ability of the flux to dissolve oxides for a longer period and at higher temperatures.

> **Safety alert:** The black fluxes are actually dark brown in color and contain fluorides, which can damage lung tissue if inhaled and should be used with good ventilation or a fume mask to protect your lungs.

2 **Support the steel**. Use firebricks, charcoal blocks or a third hand to support the steel, allowing enough room below it to direct the flame evenly across the entire surface of the back.

3 **Heat the flux**. Using a low reducing flame, heat the steel from below until the flux becomes sticky.

4 **Place the pallions**. Using pointed tweezers, pick up each pallion and place it on the steel. The spacing of the pallions depends on the desired coverage. If a translucent layer of gold is desired—in other words, with sections of steel showing through—space the pallions further apart. For a heavier more consistent layer of fused gold, place the pallions closer together.

5 **Fuse the metal**. Using a large torch tip with a **neutral flame** beneath the metal, heat until the pallions stop moving and are firmly anchored in the flux. Then, still heating from below, increase to a hot oxidizing flame and concentrate the hottest part of the flame beneath one area below the pallions. Although the steel will turn orange from the heat, it is in no danger of melting and the flame should remain focused until the pallions melt. Move to the next area and continue in this manner until all the pallions have melted. It is difficult to see exactly where the melted metal flows, but over time the ability to sense the movement of the molten gold across the surface will become more intuitive.

Step 1—If you are using a dual gas torch for fusing, start the process by applying flux to the front and back of the metal.

Step 2—Support the metal to allow you to use your torch to heat from below.

Step 3—Heat the flux with a reducing flame until it becomes sticky.

Step 4—Using sharp pointed tweezers, place the pallions onto the fluxed metal.

Step 5—After the pallions have stabilized in the flux, increase your torch to an oxidizing flame. Hold the flame beneath one area. As the pallions melt, move your torch to another area and continue until all of the pallions have melted.

Using an Acetylene/Ambient Air Torch

An acetylene/ambient air torch also works well for fusing, but the process is a bit different than with a dual gas torch. Initially, I attempted to use an acetylene/air torch for fusing following the process described. Unfortunately, the gold balled up and refused to flow so I decided to experiment with a different approach. I placed the metal pallions directly on the steel without using flux. I cranked my acetylene/ambient air torch up to a rip-roaring flame and aimed it straight down on the pallions, expecting the flame to simply blow them away. To my surprise, the hot fuel-rich flame pinned the pallions in place. I continued to hold the flame steady even when the steel turned bright orange. As in the past, the gold balled up but, rather than stopping as I had in the past, I set my jaw and kept the heat on. Finally, after what seemed like an eternity, the metal reached the appropriate temperature and flowed across the surface. Once the first few pallions melted, the others then followed quickly. As a bonus, the flow seemed to be smoother than with a fuel/oxygen torch and the buildup of scale somewhat less.

From this experiment, I concluded that an acetylene/ambient air torch works quite well. The concentrated fuel-rich flame creates a reducing atmosphere, which helps resist oxidation while the metal is brought up to the appropriate temperature. Although acetylene is a hotter fuel than propane, the heat of an acetylene/air torch is concentrated in the middle of the flame requiring a longer time for the metal to reach the appropriate temperature for fusing. Once that temperature is met, however, the melting process is quick and complete. Here are the steps for using an acetylene/air torch:

1 **Place the metal**. Place the cleaned steel on a soldering board or hard charcoal block. Do not apply flux.

2 **Place the pallions on the metal**. Using tweezers place the pallions of gold directly on the steel. The spacing you choose for the pallions will depend on the desired coverage. If a translucent layer of gold is desired—in other words, with sections of steel showing through—space the pallions further apart. For a heavier more consistent layer of fused gold, place the pallions closer together.

3 **Heat from above the steel**. Using a large torch tip with an oxidizing flame, aim it directly down on the metal pallions. Hold the flame in place until one or a few of the pallions ball up. Patience…. keep the torch in place and wait until one or more the pallions suddenly melt and flow. Once a pallion or two flow, the others should quickly follow by balling up and flowing across the steel. Although it is difficult to follow the progress of the melted metal across the steel, a slight outline will be discernable.

Step 1–Place the steel directly on a soldering board or hard charcoal block. No flux is needed.

Step 2–Using sharp pointed tweezers, place the pallions onto the fluxed metal.

Step 3–Using a large torch tip, aim the flame directly at the metal and heat one area until the pallions melt. Then move across until all have melted. Be patient. The process takes longer with an acetylene/air torch than with a dual gas torch.

Using a MAPP Gas Torch

MAPP gas consists almost entirely of propylene (not to be confused with propane) and is a colorless gas with a faint petroleum odor. A MAPP gas torch can be used to fuse metals to steel, but the results are less consistent than with a fuel/oxygen or acetylene/ambient air torch. The portable MAPP gas canisters offer flexibility for studios that cannot accommodate full size compressed gas tanks. A common disadvantage is the need to hold the MAPP canister while using the torch to fuse, a rather awkward maneuver. However, a torch and hose extension available for MAPP gas solves this issue. Here are the steps:

- **Apply flux**. Apply flux to the top surface of the steel and heat it with a reducing flame until the flux is sticky.

- **Place the pallions**. Place the pallions on the surface, spacing them as described previously in this section.

- **Fuse the metal**. MAPP gas seems to work better if the heat is applied from the top. Using a neutral flame, heat until the pallions quit moving around and then use an oxidizing flame to fuse them as described previously.

I have used a MAPP gas torch for fusing, but the results have not always been successful. Using a torch hose extension makes it easier to control your flame, increasing the likelihood of success.

Using an Enameling Kiln to Boost the Heat

Using a small benchtop enameling kiln in combination with a torch boosts the heat and can improve the flow of fused metal across the surface of the steel. If you feel your torch is not producing enough heat, the kiln may give you the boost you need. Here are the steps:

 Safety alert: Benchtop kilns can become very hot and it is a good idea to wear heat proof gloves to protect your hands. In addition, wear #3 or #4 welding glasses to protect your eyes from the bright orange glow of fused metals.

1 **Prepare the kiln**. Place the kiln on a heat proof surface with the opening directed away from your face. With the lid closed, pre-heat the kiln to its maximum temperature.

2 **Apply flux and place pallions**. Before placing the steel directly on the heating element, apply flux to the top surface in the area where you intend to fuse the metal. Then using sharp pointed tweezers, place the metal pallions on the fluxed steel. Finally, using tweezers place the steel sheet directly on the heating element of the kiln and replace the lid.

3 **Allow the metal to heat**. Allow the metal to heat for a few minutes until the flux is sticky and the pallions are stabilized.

4 **Use your torch to melt the pallions**. Using an oxidizing flame, heat the metal until the pallions melt and flow across the surface of the steel. Keep the flame directed away from the heating element of the kiln to avoid damaging it. Remove the metal from the kiln, allow it to cool slightly and then place it in the pickle.

Step 1–Preheat the kiln until you can see a soft orange glow from the ceramic heating element. If you have a heat controller, set it to the highest temperature.

Step 2–After applying flux and placing the pallions, move the steel to the kiln and carefully place it directly on the heating element. Replace the lid.

Step 3–Allow the kiln to heat the metal for a few minutes until the flux is sticky and the pallions are stabilized.

Step 4–Use a torch with a sharp oxidizing flame to slowly move across the metal, melting the pallions. Avoid aiming the torch directly on the ceramic heating element which might damage it.

Fusing Other Metals and Alloys to Steel

Non-gold metals and their alloys also can be fused to steel, offering a wide range of interesting colors and effects. Some examples are shown in the following table.

NON-GOLD METALS AND ALLOYS FUSED TO STEEL			
Metal/ Alloy Tested	Composition	Hue	Surface Appearance
Copper (100% Cu)	100% Cu	Red	Somewhat rough.
Shibuichi	75% Cu - 25% Ag*	Soft silvery pink	Fairly smooth.
Shakudo	95% Au - 5% Cu*	Bright red-orange	Fairly smooth.
Electrum	50% Au - 50% Ag*	Silver, gold undertones	Somewhat rough surface, some clumping.
Bronze	92% Cu - 8% Sn	Gold, red undertones	Flows readily but the tin can burn off leaving copper.
Brass	85% Cu - 15% Zn	Gold, red undertones	Rough surface, some clumping, and the zinc often burns off leaving copper.
Fine Silver (100% Ag)	100% Ag	Silver	Forms clumps and balls that fuse.
Argentium Silver	Three grades 93.5%, 94% and 96% Ag, balance is copper and germanium (Ge). (Ed note: the 94% grade was recently added).	Silver	Forms clumps and balls that fuse but flows somewhat better than fine silver.

*typical formula but can vary.

The surface appearance comments are based on my experiences and observations. Results can vary because many factors affect the flow and appearance of fused metals, including the amount of heat applied, the types of gases used, whether flux is present, type of flux, cleanliness of the metal and smoothness of the metal.

Shibuichi and shakudo, two Japanese alloys listed on the chart, are favorites of mine for fusing. Shibuichi, which is an alloy of copper and silver (typically 25 percent silver but this percentage can vary widely) fuses smoothly across the steel revealing a lovely rose-tinted silver veil across the surface. Shakudo, an alloy of mostly copper with a small addition of gold, flows smoothly and produces a bright coppery gold glint across the surface of the steel.

Electrum, an alloy of gold and silver, occurs naturally and can also be alloyed. I prefer a 50/50 mix of gold and silver, which flows in varying manners, sometimes smooth and even, other times rather rough. The color of electrum is an elegant gold-tinted silver.

Both brass and bronze can be fused successfully to steel; however, because of their high copper content, avoid overheating or only the copper will be evident.

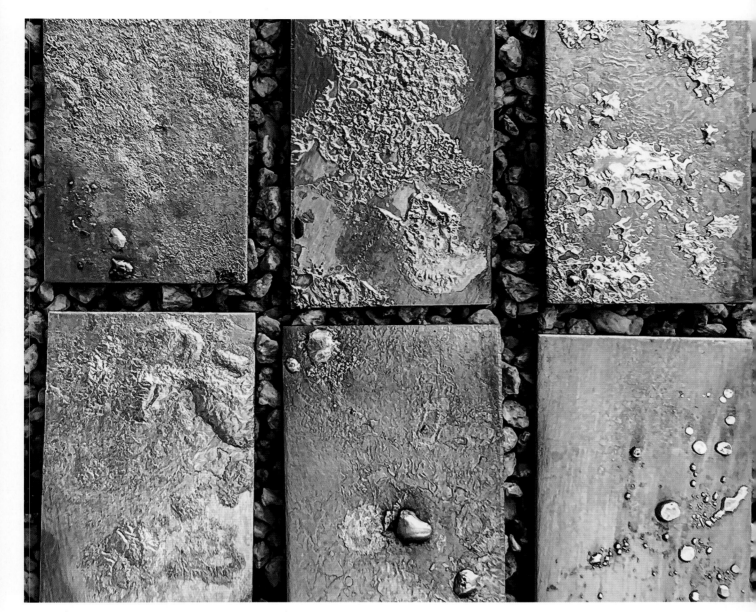

Alternatives to gold alloys fused to steel. Top row left to right: copper, brass, electrum. Bottom row left to right: shibuichi, Argentium silver and fine silver.

Fine silver and any silver alloys containing approximately 50 percent or more of fine silver (including Argentium) tend to fuse in an entirely different manner than other metals. When fused to steel, silver-based metals consolidate into balls or clumps rather than flowing across the surface. This reaction occurs because the crystalline structures of iron and silver are incompatible to the point that they resist diffusion (i.e., atomic interaction). Increasing the heat helps overcome the resistance and improves the result.

When I first began fusing silver and silver-based alloys to steel, I was frustrated by the failure of the metal to flow smoothly. As I worked more with the silver-based metals, I began to understand that the way silver and its alloys fuse to steel has a beauty of its own. The clumps or balls of fused metal resemble stars against a night sky. Also, using a rolling mill to flatten the fused silver creates a lovely dot pattern across the surface.

Silver and silver alloys tend to consolidate when fused to steel, resulting in clumps or balls across that surface.

After fusing silver to steel, you may choose to flatten the clumps and balls by rolling it through the rolling mill.

Controlling the Flow of Fused Metals

During the fusing process, the gold or other metals/alloys flow randomly across the steel. Many factors affect where the metal flows, including the type of metals, the type of torch used, use of flux, amount of heat and the shape of the piece.

If you want to restrict the flow of the fused metal to specific areas, there are several techniques that can be used. First, yellow ochre or masking mud can be painted in a thin coat onto areas where you do not want the metal to flow. Yellow ochre is readily available in powdered or liquid form from art supply stores or Amazon. Masking mud can be purchased from jewelry suppliers. Allow the ochre or mud to dry thoroughly and then proceed with the fusing process. In this manner, you can control where the fused metal will flow, but it is not possible to achieve an exact delineation.

Another technique for controlling the flow is to use a hot torch to draw the melting metal across the surface, like solder can be drawn by heat. Adding gravity to the mix is also helpful. Simply use the shape of a piece or tilt it at an angle to allow the fused metal to flow downward.

Here, yellow ochre has been applied in areas to restrict the flow of fused metals. The ochre or masking mud should be dried thoroughly before continuing with the fusing process.

A torch can be used to draw the molten metal across the surface.

Using gravity is another way to "guide" the flow of molten metal across the surface of the steel.

Quenching

After fusing metal to steel sheet, it's a good idea to allow it to cool slightly before quenching it in water. Although mild steel sheet does not contain enough carbon to become brittle, the carbon and the fuel gas will form carbon monoxide, which reacts with iron and allows the carbon to split off and diffuse into the iron. This creates a carbon enriched case on the surface but does not harden the steel.

Removing Oxidation

Traditional acids work fine for pickling steel or steel mixed-metals, including commercially available sodium bisulfate, vinegar, citric acid, muriatic acid and others. I have found that sodium bisulfate works a bit more quickly than the others.

You should maintain separate pickle containers for non-ferrous and ferrous /ferrous mixed-metals jewelry. If ferrous and non-ferrous metals are combined in an acid solution, the non-ferrous metals can become copper plated. This reaction occurs when the pickle becomes sufficiently saturated with copper and the steel produces an electrical reaction that plates the metal in a thin layer of copper.

Steel oxidizes heavily and can build up considerable scale. Thus, it requires more time to be cleaned in an acid solution than non-ferrous metals, typically a half-hour or even longer, to remove the surface oxidation and scale from steel that has been fused. I check it every 15 to 20 minutes, give it a good scrub with a brass brush and pumice cleaner and then place it back in the pickle until it is clean.

A separate pickle pot should be maintained for ferrous or mixed-metals ferrous jewelry. Non-ferrous metals will become copper plated if they are combined with any iron or steel.

Sometimes, scale will be so deeply embedded that the acid will not remove it completely. In this case, an abrasive wheel can be used to selectively abrade off the oxidation without removing the fused metal. Note too that pitting on the back of the steel is common with fuel/oxygen torches because of the intense heat. If desired, the pitted area can be sanded smooth.

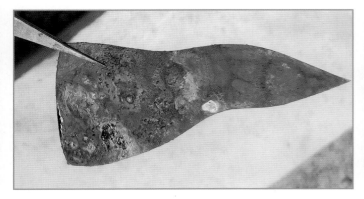

Steel oxidizes dramatically and builds up a heavy layer of scale. Removing the oxidation requires more time in the pickle than for non-ferrous metals.

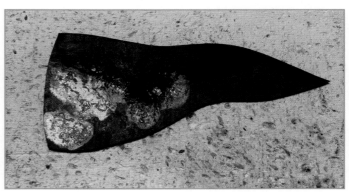

This piece has been in the pickle for 15 minutes. As you can see, it needs more time to remove the built-up oxidation and scale.

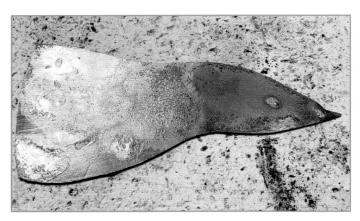

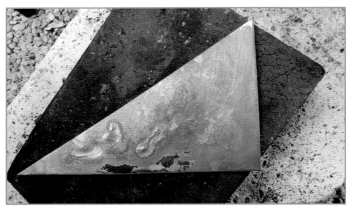

After 30 minutes, the piece is nearly clean; however, some of the stubborn oxidation remains.

Pitting can be caused by the intense heat of a dual gas torch and can be sanded if desired.

Copper Plating

Steel jewelry that has been fused with non-ferrous metals will become copper plated as copper ions are dissolved in the acid solution. The steel will cause any copper suspended in the solution to be deposited as a film of copper on the surface of the metals. Usually, this copper plating can be removed with a brass brush and pumice cleaner. If that process is not successful, a solution referred to as "super pickle" can be used very effectively. To mix super pickle combine equal small amounts of white household vinegar and hydrogen peroxide (three-percent solution). Warm the solution slightly and submerge the plated metal in it until the plating is dissolved. The super pickle may bubble and fizz as it works. After the plating is gone immediately remove the metal from the super pickle. Otherwise, the metal will re-plate and even etch if left in the solution too long.

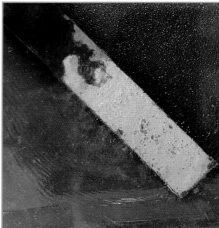

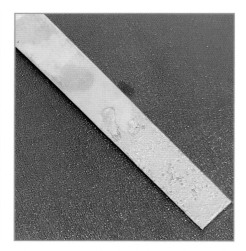

Copper plating is common with mixed-metals steel jewelry.

Placing the copper plated piece in a solution of super pickle to easily remove any copper plating. The solution will fizz a bit as the copper is removed.

The super pickle is highly effective for removing copper plating, but it is a single use solution. After it is used, the spent solution can be poured into the ferrous pickle pot.

Super pickle is effective only for a single use because hydrogen peroxide (H_2O_2) releases one of its oxygen molecules during the process and reverts to water (H_2O), leaving a vinegar and water solution, which can be safely poured into your steel pickle solution.

Order of Operations

Fusing metals to steel requires heat that is higher than the melting temperature of solders. Therefore, soldering operations, such as bezel and clasp attachments, should be done *after* fusing to avoid reflowing the joins during the fusing process. There are exceptions, particularly if the fusing occurs in areas that are fairly separated from solder joins and care is taken not to overheat the joins.

Forming can be done either before or after fusing. I like to fuse before forming, either to a blank or uncut sheet. Steel that has been fused with other metals can be formed without concern about damaging the fused surface. Texturing with hammers, chisels, burs or the rolling mill can be done either before or after fusing, but the texture will be more visible if applied after fusing.

Fusing Multiple Metals and Alloys

Combining fused metals is a wonderful way to achieve different coloration effects. When combining metals, they should be fused sequentially, according to melting temperature, from highest to lowest.

MELTING RANGE OF SELECTED GOLD ALLOYS[10]					
Karat	**% Au**	**% Ag**	**% Cu**	**Hue**	**Melting Range °F (C°)**
24	100	-	-	Yellow	1947 (1064)
22	91.7	5.5	2.8	Yellow	1823–1868 (995–1020)
22	91.7	3.2	5.1	Dark yellow	1767–1800 (964–982)
21	87.5	4.5	8.0	Yellow-pink	1724–1767 (940–964)
21	87.5	1.75	10.75	Pink	1702–1746 (928–952)
21	87.5	-	12.5	Red	1699–1724 (926–940)
18	75.0	16.0	9.0	Pale yellow	1643–1688 (895–920)
18	75.0	12.5	12.5	Yellow	1625–1643 (885–895)
18	75.0	9.0	16.0	Pink	1616–1625 (880–885)
18	75.0	4.5	20.0	Red	1634–1643 (890–895)

Melting Temperature of Non-gold Metals and Alloys

Fine silver 1762°F (961°C)
Sterling silver 1640°F (893°C)
Argentium 1580°F (860°C)
Shibuichi (60Cu/40Ag) ≈ 1688°F (920°C)
Shakudo (95Cu/5Au) ≈ 1967°F (1080°C)
Bronze (90Cu/10Sn) ≈ 1750°F (950°C)
Brass 1710°F (930°C)

Begin by fusing the metal with the highest melting temperature. Then, after cleaning the steel, paint yellow ochre or masking mud over the fused metal to avoid remelting it during the next round of fusing. Allow the ochre or mud to dry thoroughly before fusing. In this manner, it is possible to place different fused metals adjacent to one another with a discernible difference between them.

This neck piece includes shibuichi fused on the left, 18k green gold in the center and 18k red gold on the right.

The color differences are subtle and often difficult to distinguish during the work processes. This is because changes in reflective light, heat, patinas and other chemicals may temporarily "disguise" the true color. However, once the piece is thoroughly cleaned and finished, the color differences are considerably more identifiable.

Fusing to Wire, Perforated Sheet and Mesh

Through my explorations into alternative forms of steel I have found that gold and other metals can be fused successfully to steel wire, perforated steel sheet, expanded steel sheet and woven steel mesh. Each of these forms has its specific requirements, but the overall advantages of mild steel as a material for jewelry apply across all of them.

Fusing Gold and Other Metals to Steel Wire

Fusing gold or other metals to black annealed steel wire is a beautiful way to enhance the overall appeal of the jewelry. Wire with fused metals can be used in many ways as a design element, including dressing up neck wires and wire bangles.

The order of operations depends on how you are using the wire in your design. For neck wires, bangles, and pieces constructed of wire, I like to form them first and then fuse the metal in certain areas to complement the design. For wire that will be incorporated into a larger piece, for example, wire that is integrated into pierced areas, I fuse the metal first and then cut, form and solder it where needed.

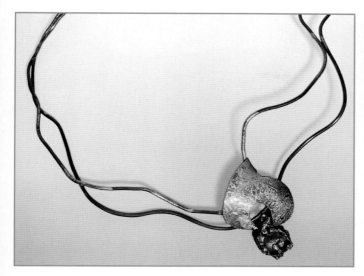

With wire neck pieces, I typically form the wire before fusing metals to it. Doing this I can determine the exact placement of the fused metals.

When using wire as part of a design, I typically form the wire after fusing metals to it, which is the approach that I used for this cuff which incorporates wire into the pierced opening.

Fusing metal to steel wire requires much less heat than with steel sheet. In fact, with too much heat you will risk melting or breaking the wire. The amount of heat you should use depends on the thickness of the wire. Here are the steps for fusing gold or other metals to low carbon steel wire:

1 Clean the wire. Begin by scrubbing off the dark coating with pumice cleaner and wiping the wire with alcohol. If you are working with a long piece of wire, it is helpful to coil it into an open spiral.

2 Flux the wire. Flux the wire in areas where you want to fuse the metal.

3 Place the pallions. Using pointed tweezers, pick up and place the metal pallions on the fluxed areas, using the flux as a glue to hold the pallions in place against the wire. It doesn't matter whether the pallions are placed on top, below or leaning against the wire as long as they are in contact with it. Fused metal tends to consolidate into clumps on wire, so it is a good idea to allow space between groups of pallions. The fused metal will wrap around the wire providing full coverage.

4 Heat the wire. Using a neutral flame, heat the wire until the flux has become sticky and the metal pallions have stopped moving.

5 Fuse the metals. Direct the hottest point of the flame on the first group of pallions and when the metal has melted and flowed, move on to the next. Continue in this manner until all the pallions have melted.

6 Cool slowly. Place the wire in vermiculite or sand and allow it to cool slowly to avoid case hardening, then pickle and clean. Case hardening occurs when the wire absorbs carbon and hardens slightly, which leads to brittle behavior. As a result, wire can bend or possibly break if it is quenched immediately.

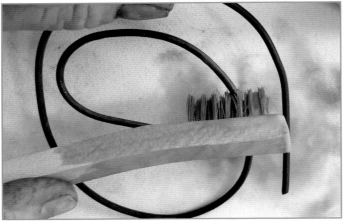

Step 1–Scrub the dark coating off the wire and then wipe it with alcohol.

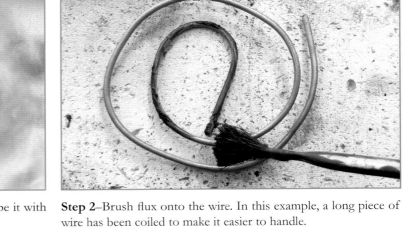

Step 2–Brush flux onto the wire. In this example, a long piece of wire has been coiled to make it easier to handle.

Step 3–Using sharp tweezers, place the pallions on, underneath or leaning against the wire. The wet flux will help hold the pallions in place.

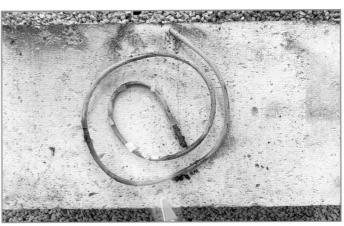

Step 4–Use a low reducing flame to gradually heat the flux until it has become sticky and the pallions are stabilized.

Step 5–Increase the heat and hold the flame on the first group of pallions until they are melted and flow across the wire. Be careful to control the amount of heat so you don't melt the wire. Move along the wire with your flame until all of the pallions are melted.

Step 6–Immediately place the wire into a container of vermiculite or sand to slow the cooling process. If the wire is quenched before cooling, it can case harden and become brittle.

Fusing Gold and Other Metals to Perforated and Expanded Steel Sheet

The fusing process for perforated and expanded steel sheet will depend on the pattern, specifically the amount of open area and corresponding amount of mass of the steel. For patterns with a lot of open area and little mass, such as the hexagon pattern, the process will be similar to fusing metals to wire, as described in the previous section. Be sure to use less heat with the thinner patterns to avoid melting the steel. For patterns that have more mass and less open area, the process will be similar to fusing metals to solid sheet, as described earlier in this chapter.

If you are fusing metals to perforated steel that has a lot of open area, such as this hexagonal pattern, use the same process as you would for fusing to wire. Keep the flame low enough so that it does not melt the delicate wires forming the perforated steel.

If you are fusing metals to perforated steel that has more mass, such as this sheet with a circle pattern, use the same process as you would for fusing to solid sheet.

Fusing Gold and Other Metals to Woven Steel Mesh

Fusing gold to woven steel mesh can be tricky because of the delicacy of the mesh. Mesh is simply a series of woven wires and should be treated in the same way as wire when fusing metals to it. Coarser mesh offers the best opportunity for achieving a successful flow of fused metal. A surprisingly low amount of heat is needed to fuse metals to steel mesh, so start with a reducing to neutral flame and move across the mesh as the metal fuses. As with wire, allow the woven steel mesh to cool completely in a bed of vermiculite or sand before placing it in the pickle.

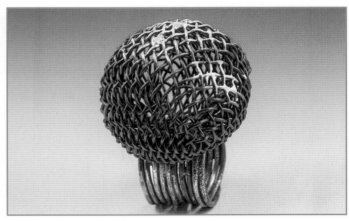

Surprisingly little heat is needed to fuse metals to woven steel mesh. Here I am using a relatively small flame to fuse gold to this fine woven mesh sphere. With an even finer mesh, I would dial down my flame considerably.

The fused gold adds a level of allure and sophistication to this simple mesh sphere ring.

Troubleshooting

- **The non-ferrous metals will not fuse or flow**. Insufficient heat is the most common reason for this problem. If the heat is too low, oxidation and scale accumulate and build a barrier that prevents the non-ferrous metal from flowing across the surface of the steel. In this case the metal either remains in pallion form or consolidates into a ball and remains on the surface of the steel. If this occurs, pickle and scrub the steel until the oxidation is removed and then try again. Another reason might be that the steel has not been cleaned thoroughly, in which case, the cleaning process should be repeated before fusing is again attempted.

- **Fused metal is too thin and spotty**. If the fused metal is not as thick or even as desired in certain areas, the fusing process can be repeated after the steel has been pickled and cleaned. Simply place pallions in the thin spots and follow the fusing process. If the fused metal seems to be heavily consolidated in some areas, yet too thin in others, it can be re-flowed.

- **Fused metal has flowed to unwanted areas**. If fused metal has flowed to areas where it is not wanted despite having used a masking material as previously described, the errant metal can be removed using an abrasive wheel.

- **Fused metal is lumpy**. Keep in mind that some metals produce a lumpier surface than others after being fused to steel. If you wish, you can remelt the metal to see if that produces a smoother surface. If the surface of the fused metal is still too lumpy, even after reflowing it, the piece can be rolled through the rolling mill using light to moderate pressure. This will smooth the surface of the fused metal.

A Word on Galvanic Corrosion

When fusing gold or other metals to steel, it is possible for **galvanic corrosion** (aka **bimetallic corrosion**) to occur over time. Although galvanic corrosion is an interesting phenomenon and can occur with mixed-metal steel jewelry, it is highly unusual.

Galvanic corrosion is an electrochemical process where one metal corrodes when it is in contact with another and an electrolyte such as water or sweat is present. Different metals have different levels of electrical conductivity and when two or more come in contact in the presence of an electrolyte, one metal acts as an anode and one as a cathode, so the two metals produce a current like a battery. This process results in an electrical attack on the anode metal, dissolving it over time. Carbon steel is rated higher toward the anode end of the scale with a rating of -0.440, while gold is rated toward the cathode end of the scale with a rating of +1.42. This means that it is possible over time for the steel to corrode and be dissolved leaving the gold.

An interesting example of galvanic corrosion occurred with the Statue of Liberty. Regular maintenance checks in the 1980s revealed that galvanic corrosion had eroded the wrought iron support structure, requiring a complete disassembly and reassembly of the statue. The armature of the statue was replaced using stainless steel coated with non-stick Teflon®, which solved the problem.

Replacing the armature of the Statue of Liberty in the mid-1980s after it was discovered that galvanic corrosion had caused severe damage.

6. FUSING POWDERED METALS TO STEEL

OVER THE YEARS, AS I experimented with fusing metals to steel, I began to wonder whether the size of the pallions might affect how smoothly the fused metal flows across the surface of the steel. Cutting the gold pallions into smaller sizes did indeed result in a smoother flow, but the process of cutting and placing tiny pallions was very tedious. It occurred to me that non-ferrous metals in powdered form might be a reasonable alternative to the pallions.

I have not yet found a source for purchasing gold powder. However, gold flakes, which are created by grinding gold leaf, are commercially available and are often used in Japanese art, including kintsugi, which involves repairing broken pottery with lacquer that has been dusted or mixed with the flakes. Gold flakes are also used as an edible element in high-end culinary preparations. Commercially available 24k gold flakes are sold by the gram or partial gram and are extremely expensive, often 50 to 100 percent higher than the market price of gold.

Powdered metals have many applications in industry, including auto manufacturing and health care. They are produced by first **smelting** a metal or alloy, removing the dross and then passing the molten metal through a nozzle. A gas is introduced just before the metal leaves the nozzle, causing extreme turbulence, which causes the molten metal to break into tiny, atomized particles. Most metal powders are available in approximately 325-mesh.*

3D printing with powdered metals is a relatively new and exciting manufacturing development. The process of creating jewelry from powdered metals using 3D printing is still emerging but there are a number of jewelry firms which are mass producing items such as chains and findings with this process.

Back row, left to right: powdered copper, white bronze and brass. Front row: silver, gold.

*Mesh size is used in the U.S. to measure the size of particles, using a sieve or screen. In this case, the number refers to a screen with 325 openings per inch.

Advantages of Powdered Metals

Powdered metals offer some exciting advantages for fusing to steel. The first is efficiency. Powdered metals are ready to go and do not require the preparation that other forms require. Also, powdered metals are a bit easier to control and place in the areas where you want fusing to occur. Most importantly, powdered metal grains fuse more quickly than metal pallions and spread more evenly across the surface of the steel. This means if you are looking for a more even layer of gold or other fused metals, powders will help you achieve that objective.

Grinding Gold Powder

Because of the high cost of gold flakes, I decided that a better option would be to grind my own powder. Although creating powdered gold is labor intensive, the result is well worth the effort. There are many different approaches for grinding gold into powder, but here are two that I have used successfully, each involving the use of a rotary flex shaft tool. For each method, I recommend starting with gold wire that is approximately one to three-inches (25 to 76 mm) long in the karat of your choice. The wire should be 14-gauge or thicker.

> **Safety alert:** Wear a particulate mask to protect your lungs while grinding metal powders.

Method 1—Grinding Wheel

Insert an aluminum or silicon carbide grinding wheel into the flex shaft. Mount the flex shaft horizontally into a vise using a strip of leather to hold it firmly in place. The grinding wheel should be facing your non-dominant hand.

Place a small funnel into the neck of a small jar and then place it directly below the grinding wheel. Then, using the foot pedal, turn the flex shaft slowly, holding the wire against the grinding wheel. As you slowly grind the wire, the fine powder will fall into the jar. Keep the flex shaft rotating at a slow speed to avoid dispersing the powder into the air.

Another approach is to use a small plastic bottle with a neck that will accommodate the grinding wheel. Cut a slot into the side of the bottle, insert the wire into the slot and hold it against the grinding wheel as you rotate the flex shaft. The powder will be trapped in the bottle.

A leather strap is useful for holding the flex shaft horizontally in a vise.

Method 2—File

Place the gold wire into a flex shaft. Hold a coarse file in your non-dominant hand and brace it horizontally against your bench on top of a sheet of heavy glossy paper. Using the foot pedal begin rotating the flex shaft *slowly* while holding the wire against the file. The gold powder will fall to the paper and can then be emptied into a small container. Glossy paper is used in this case because it helps the powder slide across the surface and into the container.

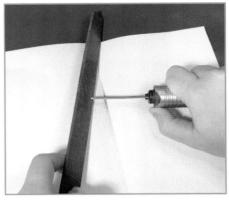

Place a grinding wheel in the flex shaft. Secure the flex shaft horizontally in a vise with the wheel facing your non-dominant hand. Hold the bottle in your dominant hand with the funnel below the grinding wheel. Hold the gold wire in your non-dominant hand. Grind the wire slowly as the gold powder falls into the bottle.

Another approach is to grind the wire inside the top half of a small plastic bottle over the flex shaft handpiece and hold firmly with your dominant hand. Hold the wire inside the bottle as you grind.

Another method is to insert the wire into the chuck of the flex shaft. Hold the flex shaft and use a file to grind the powder over a sheet of glossy paper.

Placer Gold Flour

In my search for commercially available gold powder, I discovered placer gold flour, which consists of fine gold nuggets that are mined from gravel, soil and sand that typically line rivers and streams. Although placer gold flour is coarser than powder, it is very effective for fusing to steel. The impurities that occur naturally in placer gold are not a problem for fusing because they burn off during the process. However, because of these impurities, placer gold is not usually a good candidate for casting.

Placer gold is mined from the sediment of rivers and streams. The nuggets come in various sizes, including fine flour, which is shown here.

Over eons many streams and rivers have carried placer gold downward, in the form of dust, flakes, and nuggets, to be deposited in the layers of sediment. Early prospectors panned for gold, but that's a slow and arduous method to recover it. Other mining methods speed up the process, including sluicing, which involves flowing the water through a series of troughs that agitate the slurry of gravel and water allowing the gold to fall out. Hydraulic mining is another method, which involves using a heavy spray of water to remove the soil and rock from placer gold deposits. In addition, large-scale mining of placer gold can be done using mechanical dredges.

Most placer gold has a purity between 60 to 95 percent. Australia is especially known for the purity of its natural gold, which can reach 95 percent or more. Most gold in the United States falls in the range of 70 to 80 percent or somewhere in the range of 18 to 20k. Placer gold flour is the smallest granule size readily available and is between 18 and 30-mesh. By comparison, window screen is approximately 20-mesh. Gold granules smaller than this are usually refined and turned into bars or bullion.

How to Fuse Powdered Metals to Steel

The process for fusing powdered gold and other metals to steel is very similar to fusing metal pallions to steel, including the type of torch that is needed. This process is covered in detail in the previous chapter.

To melt the non-ferrous metals you will need a flame that is hot enough such as dual gas (oxygen plus propane, acetylene or natural gas) or an acetylene/air torch. Smaller, single gas torches such as butane or propane, do not produce sufficient heat.

Here are the steps:

1 **Clean the steel**. Scrub the steel thoroughly using pumice cleaner and a stiff wire brush until water sheets off the metal. Then scrub it with a mesh scrub pad or steel wool to slightly roughen the surface (referred to as giving it tooth). Finally wipe the metal with alcohol.

2 **Flux the metal**. Any flux will work but I prefer to use a brazing flux because it remains active longer than standard fluxes. Apply the flux to the area where you want the powdered metal to fuse.

3 **Sprinkle the powder onto the metal**. Do this while the flux is still wet, which helps the powder adhere. You can use a small spoon, spatula or the side of a knife to carefully sprinkle the powder in an even layer across the flux. Small, individual saltshakers are another good way to sprinkle the powder onto the surface. A little powder goes a long way, particularly gold, so start with a thin layer. If the result is too sparse after the powder is fused, you can reapply after thoroughly cleaning the metal.

4 **Heat the metal.*** Use a neutral flame to gradually heat the metal until the flux is sticky and the powder is not moving around. Then increase the torch to an oxidizing flame and hold it on one area of the powder until it melts. Move to another section and continue in this manner until all the powdered metal has melted. Dual gas torches produce a more focused flame, which results in quicker melting of the fused metal. With an acetylene/air torch, the heat is concentrated in the center of the flame, which means that a bit more time will be required.

> **Safety alert:** Proper ventilation is essential when fusing metals to steel.

*When using a gas + oxygen torch, you have the option to heat from below or above the metal. If you heat from below, it is a good idea to apply flux to both sides to help avoid excess oxidation.

5 **Cool, quench and pickle**. Allow the metal to cool a bit before quenching. Then place it in the pickle. Scrub it with a stiff brass brush and pumice cleaner every 15 minutes until all oxidation is removed. If more coverage is desired, simply repeat the fusing process.

As described in the previous chapter, yellow ochre or masking mud can be used to roughly define the flow of the fused metals.

Step 1–Clean the steel thoroughly using pumice cleanser and a stiff brass brush. Then rub with a mesh pad to slightly roughen the surface. Finish by wiping the metal with denatured or isopropyl alcohol.

Step 2–Spread flux in the area where you wish to fuse the powdered metal.

Step 3–After cleaning the steel and applying flux to the surface, use a small spoon or spatula to sprinkle a layer of powder onto the flux.

Step 4–Using a neutral flame, heat the metal until the flux is sticky and the powder is stabilized. Then use an oxidizing flame to fuse the powder in one area. Move to another area and continue in this manner until all the powdered metal has fused.

Step 5–After allowing the metal to cool for a few seconds, quench it and then place it into the pickle to remove the oxidation.

How Various Powdered Metals Respond		
Powder	Composition	Behavior/Appearance
Gold	14 to 22k in various colors	Flows smoothly across the surface.
Copper	100Cu	Somewhat lumpier than other metals.
White bronze	Generally 55Cu/30Sn/15Zn	Silver in color, resists tarnish and corrosion, fuses evenly.
Brass	Generally 67Cu/33Zn	Zinc often burns off leaving a copperish color.
Silver	100Ag	Fuses in small beads across the surface.

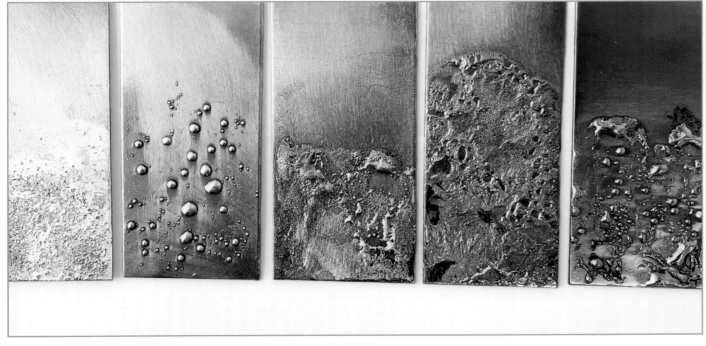

Examples of fused metals, left to right: gold powder, silver powder, copper powder, white bronze powder, brass powder.

Troubleshooting

• **Powdered metal clumps, and does not fuse**. Try using less of the powdered metal and increase the heat.

Also refer to the Troubleshooting section on page 76.

7. Keum Boo on Steel

KEUM BOO INVOLVES BONDING FINE gold or silver foil (or their alloys) to certain metals using relatively low heat and pressure. The technique also works brilliantly on steel. Fine gold or silver foil and any foils of gold/silver alloys can also be used, offering a cost-effective alternative to 24k gold.

Heating the metals increases the movement of atoms, and applying pressure causes an electron exchange at the surface resulting in **solid state diffusion** bonding of the metals.

Solid state diffusion is a process where the atoms of two solid metals intersperse themselves over time. This exchange of electrons at the atomic level occurs because metallic solids have asperities (or atomic vacancies) that allow atoms to exchange places in an attempt to achieve equilibrium. Heat increases movement of the atoms and when pressure is added this causes an electron exchange at the surface between the two metals.

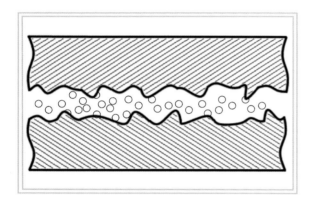

Illustration of the Keum Boo process at a microscopic level. Heat and pressure cause the atoms at the surface of the two metals to intersperse, a process called solid state diffusion bonding. This exchange at the atomic level occurs because metallic solids have asperities (or atomic vacancies as illustrated here by the jagged surfaces) that allow atoms to exchange places in an attempt to achieve equilibrium.

History of Keum Boo

Keum Boo has its original roots in ancient Rome and Greece, but the technique was fully developed in Korea, which is recognized as its birthplace. In Korea, Keum Boo has been traced back to the twelfth century Goryeo dynasty. Examples from this period have been found on acupuncture needle cases. Later examples can be traced to the Joseon dynasty (fifteenth through nineteenth centuries) where it was used inside the bowls of silver spoons and on the tips of chopsticks used by the royal court.[11] In Korea, gold foil is often bonded to finished silver objects such as jewelry, hollowware and eating utensils. Korean silver utensils and vessels are often decorated with Keum Boo, particularly inside cups, bowls and spoons so the gold will come into contact with food and imbue it with health-promoting properties.[12]

Keum Boo has also been used in other Asian countries including Japan and China. While Keum Boo is an ancient technique, in the West it wasn't until the 1980s that it began gaining much visibility. This was largely due to the efforts of a few individuals including Professor Komelia Okim, whose Senior Fulbright Exchange grants enabled her to conduct extensive research into Korean metal techniques.[13] In addition, Charles Lewton-Brain has published numerous articles, books and tutorials on the topic of Keum Boo.[14]

In the United States, Keum Boo almost exclusively involves bonding 24k gold foil to fine or sterling silver.

Using steel as the base metal is rare. I became curious about the technique in 2014 when I read a 1987 book entitled *Keum Boo: Hot Burnished Gold Foil* by Charles Lewton-Brain who raised the topic of Keum Boo on steel and commented that "*it works so well that the Koreans complain about the gold sticking to their polished steel burnishers if it gets too hot.*"[15] In addition, Celie Fago, in her 2004 book *Keum Boo on Silver: Techniques for Applying 24k Gold to Silver* wrote, "*The fact that foil sticks to the steel burnisher is a persistent curiosity that draws my interest; can gold foil be fused to steel?*"[16] After numerous tries, I discovered that gold foil can indeed be fused to steel using the Keum Boo process, producing a dramatic effect.

An example of 24k gold Keum Boo inlaying. Godfather Urn by Komelia Okim, 2016. Sterling silver and Korean Sumac Lacquering.

Advantages of Keum Boo on Steel

As I worked with various methods for bonding foil to steel, I discovered some key advantages that steel offers, including the following:

- **Depletion gilding is not required for steel**. Steel does not need to be depletion gilded as is required for sterling silver.* The foil bonds readily to clean steel.

- **Steel "signals-- the correct bonding temperature**. As steel is heated it changes colors, starting with a pale straw color, moving through tan, brown, purple, blue and other colors as the temperature increases. When it reaches the right temperature for bonding to occur (575°F/302°C) the steel turns bright blue. Note that the foil bonds to steel at a slightly lower temperature than it does to silver, which requires a temperature of roughly 700°F (371°C). As you watch the color change, you will know when to begin the burnishing process to ensure complete bonding of the foil.

*Depletion gilding is a process that involves repeatedly annealing sterling silver and then scrubbing the surface. With the final annealing, the surface is left unscrubbed and a layer of fine silver remains.

Steel Color Changes

	800°F	427°C	Dark gray
Full Bonding	575°F	302°C	Blue
	540°F	282°C	Dark purple
	520°F	271°C	Purple
	500°F	260°C	Brown purple
Bonding Begins	480°F	249°C	Brown
Start Tapping	465°F	241°C	Dark straw
	445°F	229°C	Light straw
	390°F	199°C	Faint straw

- **Steel holds up to heat**. Steel's high melting temperature alleviates concerns about melting the foundation metal. Sterling silver melts at 1650°F (899°C). Thus, if a torch is used for Keum Boo on silver, the heat must be carefully controlled to avoid melting the sterling silver base sheet. Steel, with its melting temperature of about 2600°F (1427°C) does not pose this same risk and a torch can be used to apply heat without risk of melting the base metal.

- **Steel offers more contrast with the foil**. Most patinas for steel do not appreciably affect the foil. Whether you use a black patina or another color it is easy to achieve an extreme contrast with the Keum Boo foil.

When using sterling silver as the foundation metal for Keum Boo, the silver must first be depletion gilded, a process that involves repeated annealings to reveal a top layer of fine silver. Steel does not require depletion gilding.

The blue color of the steel indicates that it has reached approximately 575°F (302°C) the correct temperature for the foil to bond successfully.

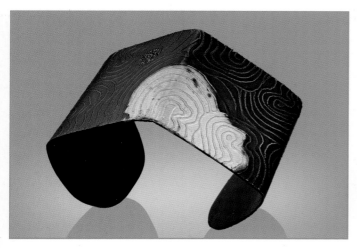

Rio de Oro cuff. Etched steel with 24k gold foil applied using the Keum Boo technique. Bette Barnett, 2015.

The patinas that affect steel do not appreciably affect the foil, resulting in a rich contrast of the metals. Tailspin earrings. Bette Barnett, 2023.

When I first began experimenting with Keum Boo on steel in 2014 I used a kitchen hot plate as the heat source. While the process worked occasionally, I was unable to consistently achieve a secure bond and the foil often peeled off in the acid bath. I determined that this problem was caused by temperature fluctuations. Nearly all kitchen hotplates (non-scientific hotplates) have a maximum temperature of around 500°F (260°C) and will automatically shut off when that temperature is reached. The hotplate then cools significantly before the heat is restarted, resulting in inconsistent results. As I continued to work, I discovered more controllable heat sources, a torch and a small tabletop kiln, which would produce consistent results.

Preparation

The steel should be thoroughly cleaned by scrubbing it with pumice based cleaner and lightly roughening its surface with a woven mesh scrub pad. Finally, wipe the steel with denatured or isopropyl alcohol. Foil can be bonded to textured steel, including hammer and roller textures, as well as an etched surface.

When I first attempted Keum Boo on steel, I used gold leaf, which is much thinner than foil and extremely fragile. My initial efforts were unsuccessful because the fragile gold leaf broke apart or was completely diffused when heat was applied.* Upon recommendations from other jewelers, I tried gold foil and began to have some success. Gold foil is readily available from metal suppliers. The ideal thickness is about 0.013 mm (13 microns) yet the thickness varies among different suppliers.

As an alternative to purchasing foil, you can prepare it in the studio using a rolling mill. Begin by rolling a 24k gold ingot into a sheet until the rolling mill is at its thinnest position, annealing when the gold becomes springy. Place the strip of gold between two larger pieces of oiled or oxidized copper sheet. The oil or oxidation will keep the gold from bonding to the copper. Keep rolling repeatedly even after you reach the thinnest setting on the rolling mill. In this manner, the gold can be rolled to the proper thickness for Keum Boo. The foil must be thick enough to handle and cut but thin enough to bond to the steel. While it is difficult to measure the right thickness, an effective comparison would be to the thickness of household aluminum foil.

*Note that leaf can be applied to steel using specialized supplies such as a gilder's sizing and a gilding cushion. However, this is not the same process that is used for Keum Boo.

Keum Boo means "gold" (Keum) and "attached" (Boo). However, gold is not the only metal foil that can be attached to steel. Fine silver foil also works well with steel. (It also works on silver but is rather pointless because there is no color differentiation.) "Eun" is the Korean word for silver and thus I have coined the term "Eun Boo" to more accurately describe the materials. Any alloy consisting of gold and silver will work for the process, including electrum, an alloy that is composed of 50 percent fine gold and 50 percent fine silver.

Foil for Keum Boo is thicker than gold or silver leaf. Be sure to source the foil from a reliable vendor.

A word of advice: As with any technique that is new to you, Keum Boo on steel can be challenging when you first attempt it. By following the steps described here, over time the process will become more familiar and you will gain a "feel" for it.

Fine silver foil also works well for this process, referred to as Eun Boo, the Korean expression for "attached silver."

You can prepare your own foil, using a rolling mill to produce a very thin sheet and repeatedly annealing the metal as it becomes springy.

Historically, in Asian countries the foil for Keum Boo was cut into intricate shapes and designs, frequently depicting scenes from nature and layered in repeated motifs. Modern designs have become more angular and contemporary. In the U.S. it is more common to use simple geometric shapes. As Keum Boo continues to become more common in the U.S., my hope is that artists here will begin experimenting with increasingly detailed and refined shapes for Keum Boo applications.

To prepare the foil for bonding, it should always be handled with sharp pointed tweezers or a fine hair brush. It is tempting to reach for an errant piece of foil without using the tweezers or a brush, but more often than not, the piece will float away or tear. Over time, using the tweezers or brush for handling the foil will become second nature.

Use a folded piece of tracing paper to hold the foil for cutting. Usually, I place a piece of foil inside the tracing paper with one edge against the fold to anchor the foil. Draw your design on a piece of paper and roughly cut out the shape. Then cut a piece of foil that is large enough to cover your drawing and place the foil inside a folded piece of tracing paper with one edge of the foil against the fold. Next, place your drawing inside the folded tracing paper covering the foil.

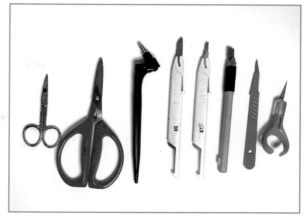

Many different types of cutting tools are helpful for Keum Boo foil, including craft knives, disposable scalpels, punches and scissors.

Some artists use double sided craft tape or   shelf paper and stick it to the foil before inserting the foil inside the folded paper. Doing this the tape or paper adheres to the foil and keeps it from slipping, making it much easier to cut the design. As the foil is bonded to the metal, the paper and residue from the adhesive are burned off.

I use a variety of cutting tools for Keum Boo foil, including craft knives with curved and straight blades, disposable scalpels, and scissors of different sizes. Craft punches are also available for purchase and can be used to easily cut simple shapes.

The key to cutting a refined design in foil is to take it slow, making tiny cuts and keeping a steady hand. As the cutting angle needs to change, turn the paper/foil rather than the cutting tool. Also, for larger designs, it can be easier to cut them in sections and piece them together when bonding to the steel. The seams will disappear when the metal bonds.

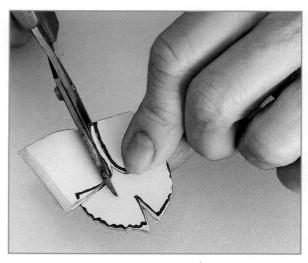

Place the foil in a folded piece of tracing paper. Draw your design on a heavier piece of paper that is wrapped over the folder and then carefully cut the shape using your preferred cutting tool.

Bonding the Foil

Keum Boo/Eun Boo on steel involves heat and pressure to achieve a secure bond. The heat source can be either a torch or a small enameling kiln. While a hotplate can work, the results are often inconsistent because most hotplates sold for kitchen use have an automatic safety shutoff mechanism that causes the temperature to fluctuate.

Be sure to have all the necessary burnishing tools at hand before applying the heat for Keum Boo. Many types of steel, tungsten carbide and agate burnishers are useful for Keum Boo and you will probably develop a preference over time. Regardless of the type of burnisher you use, be sure that it is well polished and free of any knicks or scratches, which will leave marks on the foil. In addition to burnishers, soft brass brushes are useful for bonding the foil firmly to the steel.

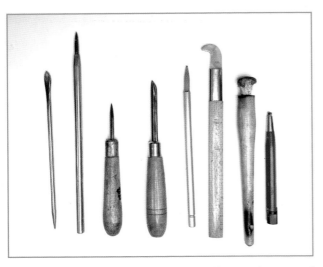

Burnishers are available in many different shapes and materials.

Steel burnishing tools will heat up as they are used, so it is important to periodically switch to a cool burnisher or keep a small container of water handy to cool the burnisher. If the steel burnisher becomes too hot, the foil will bond to it instead of the surface of the steel. With agate burnishers, there is no danger of the foil sticking to it; however, agate burnishers are fragile and will crack or break if overheated or dropped. Flame-shaped pointed agate burnishers are particularly effective for burnishing around patterns or textures.

The bonding temperature for steel (480° to 575°F/249° to 302°C) is a bit lower than it is for silver (650° to 900°F/ 343° to 482°C). There is considerable latitude between the bonding temperature and the melting temperature of the foil, allowing ample time to burnish the foil until it is securely bonded to the steel.

Using a Torch for Keum Boo

When using a torch for this process, keep in mind that very little heat is necessary and any type of torch will work, even a small butane torch. If your torch has changeable tips, you should use the smallest one available.

1 **Support the steel**. Support the steel piece firmly on firebricks or a steel grate, allowing enough room to hold the torch beneath the metal. Using tweezers or a soft paint brush dipped in water carefully pick up the foil and place it on the steel.

2 **Support the piece**. On a curved piece, it might be necessary to use diluted gum tragacanth or even saliva as "glue" to hold the foil in place. Allow any moisture to dry before applying heat.

3 **Heat and tack foil**. With a very low reducing flame, hold the torch in your non-dominant hand and begin to heat the steel beneath the area where the foil is placed. Watch as the color of the steel begins to change to a light straw moving to a darker straw color. At that point, use the flat end of a metal burnisher or rod to gently tap the foil, tacking it down onto the steel. When the bonding temperature is reached, the foil will noticeably stick to the steel. Continue to gently tap the foil as it becomes securely tacked down.

4 **Burnish**. Once the foil is securely tacked down, use a burnisher to gently smooth out any bubbles or wrinkles, starting at the center and moving toward the edges. Pay special attention to the edges to ensure they are firmly bonded. I usually start with a metal burnisher and as it becomes hot, I then switch to an agate burnisher, which I move in a light sweeping manner across the entire surface of the foil. Keep burnishing even after the foil appears to be firmly attached.

5 **Monitor heat**. If at any point the steel begins to turn a dull orange, that's a sign that the metal is getting too hot and the foil is in danger of melting. Pull the torch away from the steel until it returns to its usual dull gray color.

6 **Tap with brush**. A final step, I use the flat end of a soft-bristled brass brush (similar to a stenciling brush) to gently tap and press the foil ensuring that it is bonded into any microscopic crevices in the surface of the steel. Turn off the torch and continue to burnish as the metal cools.

Step 1–When using a torch for Keum Boo, support the piece securely with firebricks or something similar, allowing enough space to use your torch to heat from below.

Step 2–On curved pieces, you can keep the foil from sliding off by brushing the surface of the steel with a dilute solution of gum tragacanth or saliva. Allow any moisture to dry thoroughly before applying heat.

Step 3–Holding the torch in your non-dominant hand, heat from below using a reducing flame. When the steel begins to turn a pale straw color, begin gently tacking down the foil using the flat end of a steel burnisher or a metal rod.

Step 4–After the foil is tacked down, gently burnish it starting from the center and working to the edges of the foil. Keep burnishing even after the foil appears to be fully bonded. As needed, you may choose to switch to different types of burnishers during this process.

Step 5–Here the steel has overheated and is starting to turn a dull orange. If this occurs, immediately reduce the heat to avoid melting the foil.

Step 6a–As a final step, use a soft brass brush to gently tap the foil, ensuring that it is fully bonded to the steel.

Step 6b–After you remove the heat, continue burnishing the foil as the metal cools.

Using a Benchtop Kiln for Keum Boo

A small ceramic benchtop kiln, often used for enameling, provides an effective heat source for Keum Boo. If the kiln has a thermostat, set it to about 75 percent of the maximum temperature. Preheat the kiln with the lid closed.

1 **Place foil.** Using tweezers or a soft paintbrush dipped in water, carefully pick up the foil and place it on the steel. On a curved piece, it might be necessary to use diluted gum tragacanth or even saliva as "glue" to hold the foil in place. Allow any moisture to dry before placing the metal in the kiln. Place the steel piece directly on the ceramic heating element of the kiln. Note that, unlike silver, steel does not require a metal buffer sheet to be placed between it and the heating element because there is no danger of overheating the steel.

2 **Secure with tweezers.** It may be necessary to use cross-locking tweezers to hold the piece steady or to hold a pair of tweezers in your non-dominant hand to brace the piece while it is being burnished.

3 **Tap foil to tack.** Close the lid and allow the metal to heat for a few minutes, occasionally checking to see when it begins to change color. As the steel begins to turn a straw color, gently tap the foil down with the flat end of the handle of a metal burnisher or rod. Continue tapping until the foil is securely tacked to the steel.

4 **Burnish.** Use a burnisher to gently smooth out any bubbles or wrinkles, starting at the center and moving toward the edges. Pay special attention to the edges to ensure they are firmly bonded. I usually start with a metal burnisher and as it becomes hot, I then switch to an agate burnisher, which I move in a light sweeping manner across the entire surface of the foil. Keep burnishing even after the foil appears to be firmly attached.

5 **Tap with brush.** Use the flat end of a soft-bristled brass brush to gently tap and press the foil.

6 **Remove and burnish.** After the foil is firmly bonded, remove the piece from the kiln and continue burnishing as it cools.

 Safety alert: To protect your hands from the heat of the kiln, it's a good idea to wear welding gloves

Step 1–A small ceramic benchtop kiln provides a consistent heat source that is excellent for Keum Boo on steel. The metal can be placed directly on the ceramic heating element.

Step 2–It may be necessary to secure the metal using locking tweezers.

Step 3—After the steel begins to turn a straw color, begin tacking it down using the flat end of a steel burnisher or a metal rod. You may want to wear heat protective gloves.

Step 4—After the foil is tacked down, gently burnish it starting from the center and working to the edges of the foil. Keep burnishing even after the foil appears to be fully bonded. As needed, you may choose to switch to different types of burnishers during this process.

Step 5—Use a soft brass brush to gently tap the foil, ensuring that the foil is fully diffused into the asperities of the steel.

Step 6—After you remove the heat, continue burnishing the foil as the metal cools.

Finishing Up

Allow the piece to air cool for a bit. The Keum Boo process produces oxides that result in a dark heat patina. If you wish, you can allow this patina to stay without placing the piece in the pickle solution to remove it. However, the oxides are not often as even as desired in which case further patination may be required.

If you place the metal in the pickle solution, leave it only long enough to remove any oxidation. Too long in the pickle can result in the foil lifting off the surface of the steel. After 10 to 15 minutes, lightly scrub the piece with a soft brush such as a toothbrush (not a stiff brass brush) and avoid brushing over the foil.

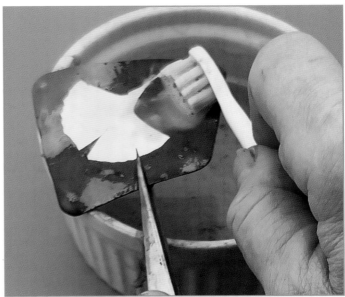

Heating the metal will result in oxidation, which does not need to be removed if you prefer.

Place the metal in the pickle solution long enough to remove the oxides. Use a soft brush, such as a toothbrush, to remove any oxides, avoiding the foil.

Layering Keum Boo and Eun Boo

Metal foils can be layered, meaning stacked in overlapping patterns, offering additional design options. Gold, silver and any gold/silver alloys can be used in the process. Several layers of foil can be burnished into place in a single operation or separately. If you add foil and heat it in separate steps, keep in mind that the layer(s) in place are likely to loosen with heat. Simply burnish over all the layers to reattach the foil firmly to the steel.

Order of Operations

Keum Boo on steel is somewhat more fragile than on silver because of the atomic differences between steel and precious metals foil. Therefore, it is recommended that all soldering and forming operations be completed first before bonding the foil. This is not a hard and fast rule as I have successfully done gentle forming of well bonded pieces after applying Keum Boo.

All stone setting, patinating and finishing should be performed after the foil has been attached.

Keum Boo on Steel Wire and Perforated Steel Sheet

Keum Boo on steel wire and perforated sheet is an exciting area that invites exploration. The process is similar to Keum Boo on steel sheet; however, it is a bit more delicate. Applying foil to wire will usually require multiple layers. Think of it as painting with gold or silver and layering coats onto the wire. It works particularly well on multiple parallel wires used as a design element.

Perforated steel sheet can also be used for Keum Boo. After bonding the foil to the steel, the perforations must be cleared of excess foil using a scalpel or craft knife. Avoid filing or abrading the foil from the perforations because that is likely to tear it and leave a ragged edge.

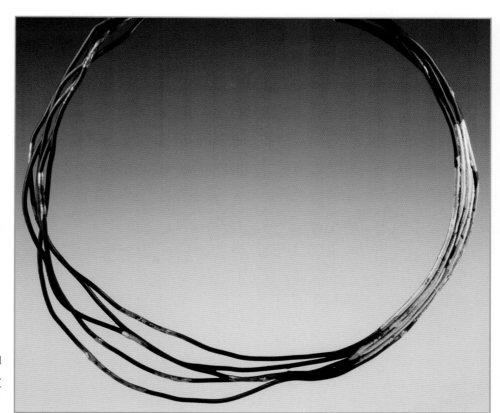

This neck piece features 24k gold foil that was burnished to parallel steel wires. The process required several layers of foil to achieve the desired coverage.

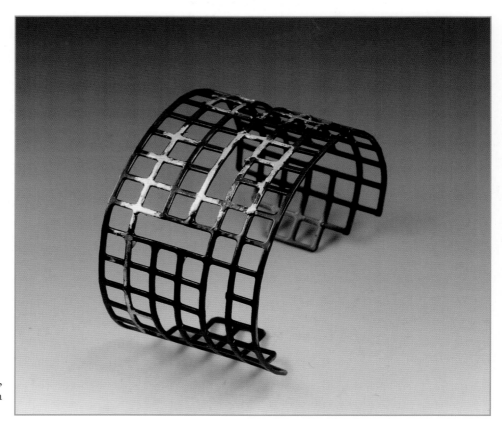

After bonding foil to perforated steel, the openings must be cleared using a scalpel or craft knife.

Troubleshooting

- **The foil tears and develops ragged edges**. Keum Boo on steel is somewhat more fragile than on silver and it is common for the foil to tear or develop ragged edges. There are some steps you can take to help avoid this situation. First, be sure that the steel is extremely clean and the foil is of the proper thickness. When the correct bonding temperature is reached, carefully and gently tack down the foil with the flat end of a burnisher or a metal rod before you begin burnishing. This helps avoid the formation of wrinkles and bubbles that can cause tearing. Finally, be sure that your burnisher is well polished and free of scratches.

  Repairing rips and tears is not difficult because the foil can be patched and the seams will blend together unnoticeably. Simply cut a patch of foil of a size that roughly covers the tear. Using tweezers place the patch over the tear. Apply heat and gently burnish the patch until it is fully bonded and undetectable.

- **The foil lifts around the edges**. If the foil lifts around the edges after it has been cleaned and pickled, it is likely that the heat and burnishing were insufficient to ensure a solid bond. Apply heat and reburnish until the lifted edges are firmly bonded.

Rips or tears in the foil can be patched and the seams will become invisible.

8 . PATINATING STEEL JEWELRY

MILD STEEL JEWELRY CAN BE enhanced by many different patinas, including a deep black that is a beautiful backdrop for fused metals and Keum Boo foils. The entire color palette is available for patinating steel, including gray, brown, yellow, orange, red, green, blue and more. Even a rust-like surface can be achieved as a stable patina on steel.

Matthew Runfola, in his book *Patina: 300+ Coloration Effects for Jewelers & Metalsmiths*, devotes an entire chapter to patinas on steel. The information is an invaluable resource for jewelers who want to experiment with the vast number of patina effects that can be achieved with steel.

In this chapter, I focus on certain patinas that I prefer for mixed-metal steel jewelry, essentially those that I feel enhance the beauty and contrast of the metals and the overall appeal of the work. However, the patinas that I describe are a mere smattering of those that are available, and I encourage you to explore any patina options that interest you.

This chapter covers two main categories of patinas: heat and chemical patinas, both of which work well on steel. A heat patina is created by changing how the surface of the metal refracts light, in other words how it separates light into various wavelengths of colors. Chemical patinas are applied to the surface of the steel and either react with it or coat it like paint.

Applying a patina is one of the last steps in creating a piece of mixed metal steel jewelry. If you are setting cabochons or gemstones, you may choose to do so before or after applying the patina, with the understanding that any scratches or marks made to the metal in the setting process will need to be touched up with additional patina. Sealing the metal, which is described in the next chapter, is the final step and is always completed after applying the patina. Before applying any type of patina, the steel must be free from fingerprints and oil. One last wipe with denatured or isopropyl alcohol is all that's needed.

Heat Patina

A heat patina works best on steel with a polished surface. A mirror finish is not necessary, but a slight polish will help produce a more even patina. Because a heat patina is produced by light that is refracted from the steel surface, the colors are delicate and difficult to preserve. This is because any slight change to the metal's surface, for example by applying a sealer, will change the way the light is refracted.

Heating steel produces different colors that change as the temperature increases. The colors move through a spectrum—from light straw to dark gray—referred to as the tempering range (see chart on page 86).

Heat patinas require fairly low temperatures and any heat source that produces these temperatures will work. However, the heat needs to be consistent and evenly applied to achieve good results. My preferred heat sources are a torch, hotplate or benchtop kiln.* For dimensional pieces of jewelry I recommend using a torch, because it is easier to control the amount of heat reaching different areas of the metal. For flat pieces, a hotplate or kiln works well because the consistent heat produces an even patina.

*A benchtop kiln is a small ceramic kiln that has a domed lid and a ceramic heating element and is often used for granulation, Keum Boo, PMC® and firing hard enamel on metal. A common brand is the Ultralite Beehive Studio Kiln.

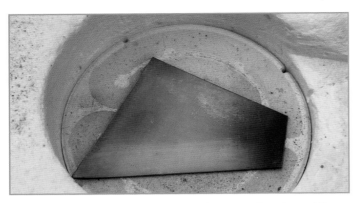

This piece of steel has been heated using a benchtop kiln to approximately 575°F (302°C) producing a bright peacock blue patina.

It is possible to achieve a deep gray, almost black, heat patina. This piece has been heated to a temperature above 800°F (427°C).

Steel is not a great conductor of heat; thus, even after the heat source is removed, the temperature of the steel will continue to rise and the color will continue to progress until the heat dissipates.

Heat Patina with a Torch

To create a heat patina with a torch, use a small torch tip and a very low reducing flame—one that is mostly yellow with a tiny bit of blue at the end. I like to heat from beneath the metal to monitor the color as it develops, but you can apply the heat from either above or below.

Support the metal on firebricks or hold it securely in locking tweezers with your non-dominant hand. Begin heating at one end of the metal and as the color develops, slowly move the torch across the metal. Remember to pull the torch away from the metal a few seconds before the desired patina is reached because the heat will continue to increase even after the flame is removed. After the desired patina is reached, immediately quench the metal in water.

Interesting patterns can be achieved with a torch patina by using a wet cotton ball held in tweezers to quickly stop the action of the heat. For example, you can create a circle pattern by holding a small oxidizing flame to one spot on the metal. As soon as the heat patina forms a circle on the surface, use the wet cotton ball to quench the metal and immediately stop further heat conduction.

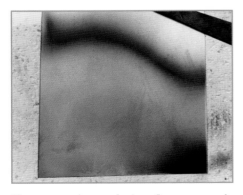

Use a very low reducing flame to apply a torch patina. Here you see a range of tempering colors as the patina begins to develop.

For pieces with considerable detail and dimension, a torch is useful to help ensure the even application of heat.

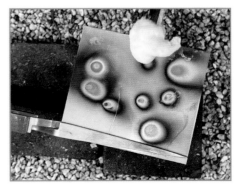

Torch patinas can be used to create patterns, such as circles, by using a wet cotton ball to stop the heating action.

Heat Patina with a Hotplate or Benchtop Kiln

A hotplate or benchtop kiln provides an even heat source. However, curved or dimensional work may develop a splotchy or streaky patina because variations in the distance of the metal from the heat source will cause it to heat unevenly. Keep in mind that most kitchen hotplates have a maximum temperature of 500°F (260°C), so it will be difficult to achieve any color beyond purple.

If you are using a hotplate, place a sheet of copper over the heating element and preheat it at the maximum temperature setting. The copper will help retain the heat if the hotplate cycles off and then back on. Place the steel piece on the copper sheet and watch as the steel moves through the tempering spectrum of colors. Remove the metal from the heat source slightly before the desired color is reached. Quench in water immediately.

If you are using a benchtop kiln that has a thermostat, preheat the kiln at a medium high setting. Without a thermostat, simply turn the kiln on and allow it to preheat until the heating element is glowing orange. Place the piece directly on the ceramic heating element and close the lid. Lift the lid approximately every 10 seconds to check the color progression. Remove the metal from the kiln shortly before the desired color is reached. Quench in water immediately.

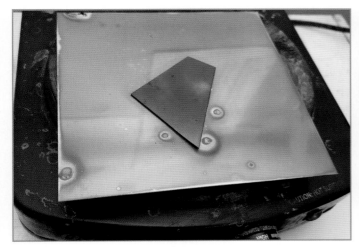

If you are using a hotplate to apply a heat patina, place a sheet of copper between the heating element and the piece to help maintain a more consistent temperature.

If you are using a benchtop kiln to apply a heat patina, when the metal begins to turn a straw color, replace the lid and then check it every few seconds. Remove the piece from the kiln shortly before it reaches the desired color.

Chemical Patinas

Some chemical patinas form naturally over time, such as the green film that forms on copper and bronze by long atmospheric exposure. A chemical patina can also be created artificially to change the surface color of the metal over a shorter period of time. In this section, I will describe chemical solutions that are formulated to artificially affect the surface of the metal.

Each chemical patina is specifically developed to affect a certain metal or group of metals. Some patinas that are designed for steel will also affect other metals, including non-ferrous metals. When you select a chemical patina, pay close attention to the metals that it will affect and avoid any patinas that will cover up non-ferrous metals that have been fused or bonded to the steel.

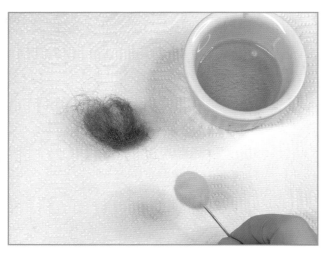

Chemical patinas can be used to create many different single and multi-color effects. Branded chemical patinas for steel are available commercially from many sources. Some colorant formulas can be mixed using chemicals and household ingredients to achieve different patina effects.

It is important to follow the instructions for application of chemical patinas, particularly the safety precautions.* Always wear gloves and ensure good ventilation (or wear a mask). Patinas can cause skin irritation and the fumes can cause headaches and respiratory problems. When working with chemical patinas, use a tray or paper towels to catch any drips because the chemicals will stain work surfaces.

When applying a chemical patina, protect your work surface with a tray or paper towels. Wear nitrile gloves and use non-reactive glass or plastic containers for the solutions.

Safety alert: Reactive blackening chemical patinas contain copper salts and other oxidants that are toxic. Be sure that you wear nitrile rubber gloves to protect your hands and that you have good ventilation.

Chemical patinas work better on steel that has been slightly roughened. Raising a slightly rough surface with a mesh scrub pad during the initial cleaning process is usually sufficient, but I sometimes use a sandblaster to achieve a matte finish early in the process in anticipation of the patina application.

Black Chemical Patinas

Several types of chemical patinas are available to achieve a deep black patina. In this section, I describe the two that I use most often: gun bluing and Sculpt Nouveau Prestoblack PC9®. These are reactive patinas, meaning the chemicals react directly with the metal and become part of it rather than simply coating it.

Gun Bluing. Gun bluing is one of the most common chemical patinas used to achieve a deep black patina on steel and can be purchased from many sources, including gun supply shops. My preferred gun bluing is sold under the name of Brownell's Oxpho Blue®; however, many brands are available.

Gun bluing creates a chemical reaction with the metal's surface selectively forming magnetite (Fe_3O_4), which is the black oxide of iron.

Here are the steps to apply most commercially available gun bluing patinas:

*Occasionally I will recommend instructions for patina application that may vary from those provided by the manufacturer. In these cases, my recommendations are based on trial-and-error experiments I preformed to discover methods that produce enhanced results for steel jewelry.

1 **Prepare**. Pour a small amount of the gun bluing directly into a small glass or plastic container without diluting it. I suggest using a wool dauber for application. Daubers are wool ball brushes with metal handles and are commonly used for dying leather.

2 **Apply the bluing**. Saturate the dauber with gun bluing and rub it across the steel in a smooth motion. You will see the steel darken immediately. After you have covered the whole surface with the patina, rub the metal firmly with fine steel wool using circular motions. This step helps even out the patina by ensuring that the chemicals are fully absorbed into the small asperities of the metal.

3 **Rinse and neutralize**. Rinse the piece in clean water, rubbing it gently with your fingers to remove any residue. If you are not satisfied with the patina, you can repeat step two until you achieve the desired result. You can apply up to three coats in this manner. After three coats, if the patina is not covering evenly, it should be removed by placing the piece in pickle and then reapplying the patina to the cleaned metal.

After rinsing the metal, place it in a weak solution of baking soda (sodium bicarbonate) and water to **neutralize** the reaction of the chemical.* Then give it a final rinse. Discard any gun bluing to avoid possible contamination rather than pouring it back into the container.

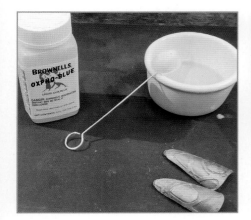  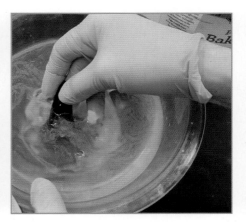

Step 1–Prepare. Here you see a small amount of undiluted gun bluing in a small glass container ready for application with the wool dauber.

Step 2–Apply the bluing. After spreading the gun bluing evenly across the metal, use a small piece of steel wool to gently rub the patina into the surface.

Step 3–Rinse and neutralize. Rinse the piece thoroughly and place it in a dilute neutralizing solution (a small amount of sodium bicarbonate in water). Then give it a final rinse and dry.

Sculpt Nouveau. Black chemical patinas can be purchased from many sources. Sculpt Nouveau, a U.S. company headquartered in Southern California, is my preferred source because of the wide variety and effectiveness of their available patinas, sealers and other surface applications for non-precious metals. The company has distributors throughout the United States and in many countries throughout the world.

Sculpt Nouveau sells several black patinas designed for iron and steel, including gun bluing-type solutions that I use regularly because they produce a rich, durable black finish. The application process is similar to the one for Brownell Oxpho Blue® but involves some slight differences in steps.

*To create the neutralizing solution add approximately one-fourth cup (23 g) sodium bicarbonate (baking soda) to two cups (473 g) of water.

1 **Prepare**. Pour a small amount of the patina into a small non-reactive plastic or glass container. Then dilute the patina with an equal amount of distilled water.

2 **Apply the patina**. Saturate a wool dauber with the diluted patina and rub it across the steel in smooth circular motions. If you prefer, you can use a spray bottle to apply the patina; however, this approach wastes a bit of the solution. You will see the steel darken immediately. After you have covered the whole surface with the patina, rub the metal firmly with fine steel wool using circular motions. This step helps even out the patina by ensuring that the chemicals are fully absorbed into the small asperities of the metal.

The instructions for Sculpt Nouveau black patinas suggest warming the metal to improve the effectiveness of the patina, but I have had better results when the metal is at room temperature. This is because steel does not conduct heat well and warming the metal produces hot spots, resulting in uneven patina coverage.

3 **Rinse and neutralize**. After applying a coat of the patina, rinse the metal in clean water. I rub the surface gently with my gloved thumbs until I can no longer feel the slippery residue from the chemical on the surface. For a deep jet-black, I repeat the process up to two more times until the patina is dense and even. After three coats, if the patina is not covering evenly, it should be removed by placing the piece in pickle and then reapplying the patina to the cleaned metal.

After rinsing the metal, place it in a weak solution of baking soda (sodium bicarbonate) and water to neutralize the reaction of the chemical. Then give it a final rinse. Discard any patina rather than pouring it back into the container to avoid possible contamination.

Step 1–Prepare. The patina is being diluted with an equal amount of distilled water before application.

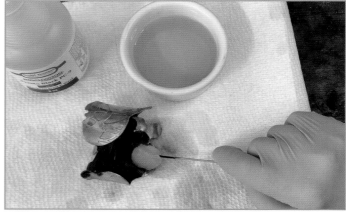

Step 2–Apply the patina. Use a wool dauber to apply the patina evenly. It is not necessary to heat the metal.

Step 3–Rinse and neutralize. Rinse the piece thoroughly and place it in a dilute neutralizing solution (sodium bicarbonate and water). Then give it a final rinse and dry.

Brown Chemical Patinas

In my view, rust is one of the most beautiful surface treatments for steel. However, for steel jewelry, rust must be stabilized and sealed to prevent further corrosion and staining. Therefore, sealing a rust patina is an essential step and will be covered in the next chapter.

Here, I will discuss two ways to achieve a rust-like patina, the first using common household items and the second using Japanese Brown®, a chemical patina available from Sculpt Nouveau. In addition, I describe how the Japanese Brown® patina can be used to create a smooth leather-like patina by changing the application method. These are also reactive patinas. The chemicals react directly with the metal and become part of it rather than simply coating it.

The beauty of a rusted surface can be achieved with steel jewelry using certain household chemicals or commercially available patina solutions.

Rust Patina Using Household Chemicals. Rust is a reddish-brown flaky coating of iron that is created through a chemical reaction called oxidation. Moisture serves as a catalyst, causing iron (the main component of low carbon steel) to lose electrons to oxygen, creating iron oxide which is the rusty coating. Acids and salts speed up the process by serving as electrolytes.

Bare mild steel rusts over time if it is exposed to moisture and air, but you can accelerate the process by using white household vinegar, hydrogen peroxide three-percent solution and table salt.

Here are the steps to create a rust patina using these common household items:

1 **Prepare**. You will need a plastic or glass spray bottle that will hold at least three cups (24 US fl oz or about three-fourths liter), a tray or paper towels to protect your work surface, white household vinegar, hydrogen peroxide three-percent solution and table salt. Pour a small amount of white vinegar into the spray bottle.

2 **Apply the vinegar**. Wipe the surface of the metal with alcohol to ensure that it is free of oils. Spray the surface of the metal with vinegar, completely covering it and then allow it to dry. Reapply the vinegar two or three times, allowing it to dry between each application. The purpose is to slightly etch the surface to react more quickly with the next solution.

3 **Mix the rusting solution**. Measure two ounces (2 US fl oz or 59 mL) of vinegar in a spray bottle. Add two cups (16 US fl oz or about one-half liter) of hydrogen peroxide and one-half teaspoon (2.5 mL) salt. Shake the bottle to mix thoroughly.

4 **Spray the metal**. After the salt has been absorbed into the solution, spray it onto the surface of the metal.

5 **Dry**. Place the metal in direct sunlight for 10 minutes or longer. You will see the rust form on the surface. If you want to increase the layer of rust, simply repeat steps four and five up to a total of four applications.

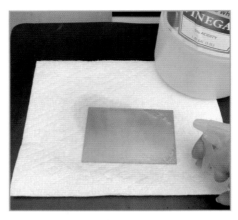

Step 1–Prepare. Gather supplies: household white vinegar, hydrogen peroxide three-percent solution and salt. Pour a small amount of household vinegar into a spray bottle.

Step 2–Apply the vinegar. Spray the piece with vinegar and allow it to dry. Repeat two or three times.

Step 3–Mix the rusting solution. Place two ounces (2 US fl. oz. or 59 mL) of vinegar in a spray bottle. Add the hydrogen peroxide and salt. Shake the bottle to mix thoroughly.

Step 4–Spray the metal. Coat the metal thoroughly with the rusting solution.

Step 5–Dry. Place the piece in the sunlight and allow it to dry at least 10 minutes. You will see the rust begin to build on the surface. You can repeat this step up to four times to increase the buildup of rust on the surface.

Rust-like Japanese Brown Patina. Japanese Brown® patina from Sculpt Nouveau is one of my favorite chemical patinas because of its ability to achieve a mottled rust-like finish or a more even leather-like one simply by changing the application method.

For a rust-like patina, Japanese Brown® is applied to room temperature metal.

Here are the steps:

1 **Prepare**. You will need a tray or paper towels to protect your work surface. Pour a small amount of the patina into a non-reactive glass or plastic container. You do not need to dilute the patina solution.

2 **Apply the patina**. Using a wool dauber or spray bottle, apply the patina solution heavily across the metal. Allow the metal to dry a few hours or overnight to allow the rust-like finish to develop.

3 **Reapply the patina**. Step 2 can be repeated three or four times until you achieve the appearance that you want. You do not need to rinse the metal between applications.

4 **Rinse and neutralize**. The written instructions for Japanese Brown® indicate that a final rinsing is not necessary, but to stop the action of the patina, I usually rinse the piece, place it in a neutralizing solution of sodium bicarbonate and water and then rinse it again before drying it.

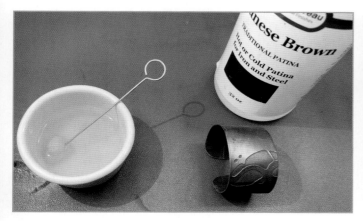

Step 1–Prepare. Here you see a small amount of undiluted Japanese Brown® patina in a small glass container ready for application with the wool dauber.

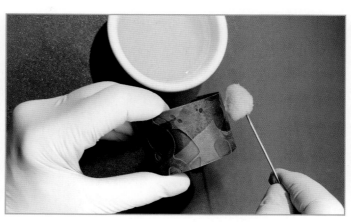

Step 2–Apply the patina. To achieve a rust-like finish, apply the patina at room temperature across the entire surface. Allow to dry at least a few hours or overnight.

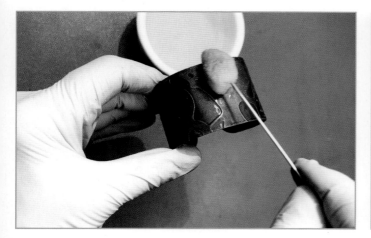

Step 3–Reapply the patina. The patina can be reapplied several times and allowed to dry each time until the desired rust-like finish is achieved.

Step 4–Rinse the piece. Place it in a neutralizing solution of sodium bicarbonate and water and then rinse it again before drying it.

Leather-like Japanese Brown Patina. For a leather-like finish, Japanese Brown® patina is applied to metal that is warmed with a heat gun.

Here are the steps:

1 **Prepare**. You will need a tray or paper towels to protect your work surface. In addition, you will need a heat gun to warm the metal and dry the patina as you apply it. Pour a small amount of the patina into a non-reactive glass or plastic container. You do not need to dilute the patina solution.

2 **Apply the patina**. Use a heat gun to warm the metal until it is approximately 200°F (93.33°C). Then use a wool dauber to spread the patina across the surface of the metal. Or if you prefer, you can use a spray bottle to apply the patina. As the patina is applied to the hot metal, it will foam a bit indicating that it is reacting chemically with the metal. Continue heating with the heat gun and as the patina dries, reapply it. You will see the color become darker and more even.

3 **Rinse and neutralize**. When you have achieved the effect you want, allow the metal to cool. Rinse it, place it in a weak neutralizing solution of sodium bicarbonate and water, and then give it a final rinse and dry it.

Safety alert: The heating element in a heat gun typically becomes red hot and can reach a temperature of 1200°F (649°C). Handle a heat gun safely by following manufacturer precautions, including:

- Do not use it around flammable materials.
- Always turn it off and allow the nozzle to cool before placing it on down on a surface.
- Do not touch the hot nozzle.
- Do not aim the heat gun toward your body or clothing.

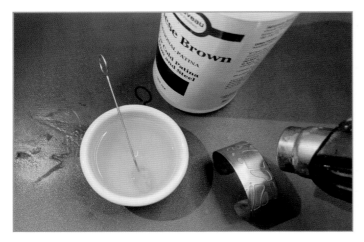

Step 1–Prepare. Using a heat gun, warm the metal before using the wool dauber to apply the patina.

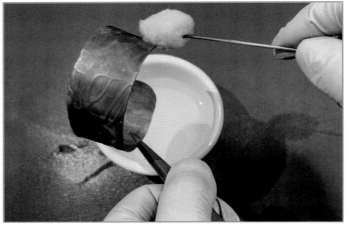

Step 2–Apply the patina. Apply the patina across the entire surface. Continue heating the metal as the patina dries until you achieve the desired leather-like finish.

Step 3–Rinse and neutralize. As a final step, rinse the metal and place the piece in a neutralizing solution. Then rinse again and dry.

Sculpt Nouveau Solvent Dyes

Solvent dyes are fast-drying, highly pigmented, solvent-based inks that are great to use on any hard surface, including metal. Once the solution is applied, the solvent evaporates, leaving a translucent application of the dye. The dye remains on the surface of the metal, meaning it does not react with the metal as do the black and brown patinas that were discussed previously in this chapter.

You can purchase a kit that includes a bottle of the solvent solution plus multiple dyes in separate small containers, or you can buy individual colors to mix with the solvent. I like to mix my own because of the flexibility I have in varying the intensity of the color.

Safety alert: Solvent dyes contain toxic and corrosive chemicals including tert-butyl acetate, which is irritating to the skin and eyes, and harmful if inhaled. Be sure to use proper ventilation and/or wear a fume mask when using. In addition, wear nitrile glove when handling.

Solvent dyes can be used on bare metal or layered over other patinas. Because the dyes are translucent, they allow any previous patina or surface color to show through, often producing very interesting effects. For example, I often layer a solvent dye over a rust-like patina to create a mottled appearance rather like tie-dying. A solvent dye can also be layered over a black patina to add a subtle hint of color.

Large angular cuff with a teal solvent dye patina layered over a rust-like Japanese Brown® patina. Fearless cuff. Bette Barnett, 2022.

Here are the steps:

1 **Prepare**. You will need a tray or paper towels to protect your work surface. Wipe the surface of the metal with alcohol to ensure that it is free of oils. Use a small glass container for the solvent dye. Pour a small amount of the solvent into the container and then add the dye. The dyes are highly concentrated and only a few drops are needed. If you want to create a custom color, you can add different dyes to the mix, a drop or two at a time, until the desired color is reached.

Safety alert: Do not use plastic containers for solvent dye solutions because solvents can easily corrode even the most resistant plastics. A glass container should be used.

2 **Apply the solvent dye.** Using a wool dauber or a small natural ocean sponge, soak it in the solution and wring it slightly against the edge of the container. Use a light dabbing motion to apply the solvent dye to the surface.

3 **Allow to dry and reapply if necessary.** Allow the solvent to dry for at least an hour. If you want a denser color, reapply the solvent dye as in step 2. Keep in mind that the solvent will dilute the first coat somewhat and the color may bleed, but that is no cause for concern.

4 **Allow to dry overnight and pre-seal.** Allow the final coat to dry overnight and then apply an acrylic based clear sealer to stabilize the solvent dye. A solvent based sealer used directly over the solvent dye would cause it to run.

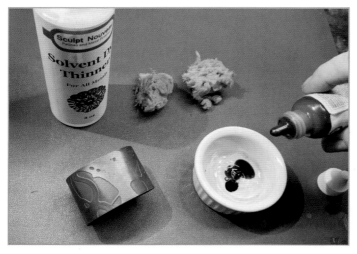

Step 1–Prepare. To mix the solvent dye patina, place a small amount of solvent in a small glass container. Add the dye to it a few drops at a time until the desired color is reached.

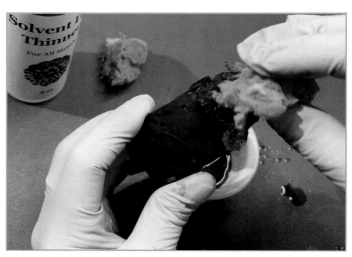

Step 2–Dab it on. Use a small natural sponge or a wool dauber to gently dab the solvent dye solution onto the surface.

Step 3–Allow to dry and reapply if necessary. After allowing the solvent dye to dry for at least one hour, you may reapply another coat if you wish to achieve a denser color. Note that each additional application will slightly dissolve the previous coats.

Step 4–Allow to dry overnight and pre-seal. After allowing the patina to dry at least overnight, stabilize the solvent dye by sealing it with an acrylic sealer. You can then add other sealers if you wish.

Patinating Soldered and Mixed-Metal Pieces

If steel jewelry has been soldered/brazed, a separate chemical patina may be needed to cover solder that shows at the join. I often use a patina for silver, such as liver of sulfur or branded patinas for silver, to mask silver solder joins in this manner.

In a similar fashion, when I combine ferrous and non-ferrous metals in a piece of jewelry, I often use different patinas for the various metals depending on my design choices. For example, I often combine reticulated silver as an element in a steel piece and may choose to apply a liver of sulfur patina to the silver and buff it back to reveal bright areas.

Sculpt Nouveau black chemical patina has been applied to the steel of this cuff, while the reticulated silver has been lightly patinated with liver of sulfur and then buffed back to reveal the highlights of the non-ferrous metal. Fidelity Cuff. Bette Barnett, 2020.

Removing Patina from Fused Metal

Patinas for steel will minimally affect gold or other alloys that have been fused or bonded to the steel. A patina may dull the non-ferrous metal and should be removed to enhance the contrast and shine. Simply use a fine silicone wheel in a flex shaft to remove the excess patina slowly and gently from the non-ferrous metal. Slowly pull the wheel toward you lightly touching it to the fused metal while keeping the RPM at the lowest level possible. It may be difficult to see where the fused metal is hidden beneath the patina, but if the raw steel is accidentally exposed in this process, it is a simple matter to touch up the naked spot with a fine brush dipped in patina.

This process can also be used to remove excess patina from foil used for Keum Boo. Chemical patinas sometimes seep under the edge of the bonded foil, giving the piece a look of antiquity. I find this look quite pleasing but excess patina should be removed from the top of the foil to brighten it.

This part of the finishing process is one of the most satisfying to me because, as the patina is removed, the glow of the non-ferrous metals is restored and the contrast is made more dramatic

A rubber or silicon wheel in the flexshaft can be used to gently remove any excess patina from fused non-ferrous metals, brightening the metal and heightening the contrast.

In the same manner, a rubber or silicon wheel can be used to brighten foil that has been bonded to the steel using the Keum Boo or Eun Boo technique.

Troubleshooting

- **Heat patina is uneven**. Usually this occurs when using a torch with a flame that is too hot, creating hot spots in the metal. It is better to use a reducing flame rich with fuel and keep the flame adjusted to a very low level. Move slowly across the metal to keep the patina even. An uneven patina can also be caused if you are using a hotplate or benchtop kiln as the heat source for a piece that is highly dimensional. In this case, the heat cannot reach the metal evenly because of the shape of the piece. Areas that are closer to the heat source will develop a heat patina more quickly than areas that are farther away. Using a torch to apply a heat patina to a dimensional piece is a better method for achieving an even color.

- **Heat patina fades when it is quenched**. Heat patinas are notoriously delicate and difficult to preserve. It is to be expected that the color will fade somewhat when the metal is quenched.

- **Heat patina is too pale**. If the patina is too pale, the heat was too low. You can intensify the color by reapplying the heat patina.

- **Black chemical patina is streaky or uneven**. This outcome can be caused by several different factors. If the metal has any oils or dirt on it, the patina may be streaky or uneven. In this case, place the piece in the pickle and then clean it thoroughly. Wipe it with alcohol and reapply the patina. Another factor might be that the metal does not have a slightly roughened surface. In this case, the patina will fail to react fully with the metal. Usually this can be resolved by reapplying the patina and, while it is still wet, using a small piece of steel wool to rub it into the surface.

- **Black chemical patina flakes off**. In this case, the usual cause is too much patina. More than three coats of patina often will result in a flaky surface. Place the piece in the pickle and scrub to remove the patina. Then reapply the patina using the process described in this chapter.

- **Japanese Brown® patina is too translucent**. If the Japanese Brown® patina is applied to room temperature metal, a translucent rust-like finish is the expected outcome. If you prefer a more opaque, even brown finish, apply the patina to warmed metal as described previously in this chapter.

Title: Primordial Cuff
Artist: Bette Barnett
Description: Steel that has been heavily electro-etched and fused with 18k yellow gold. 2023.

9 . SEALING STEEL JEWELRY

AFTER APPLYING A PATINA TO steel jewelry, it must be sealed immediately to protect it from corrosion and rust. Because chemical patinas remain active even after neutralizing them in a sodium bicarbonate and water solution, unsealed steel jewelry can begin to rust within a matter of minutes.

Modern products for sealing metals have advanced dramatically and provide a durable and long-lived finish. I have found that the three best options for sealing steel jewelry are oil, wax and lacquer. All are effective as sealers and enhance the patina by making it appear somewhat more saturated and even. It is interesting to note that when steel jewelry is worn regularly it will have greater resistance to rust because oils from the skin act as a natural sealer.

Choosing a sealer is largely a matter of practicality and aesthetics. In humid climates, a combination of sealers might be a wise choice. Regardless of the sealer(s) you choose, before application, always wipe the jewelry surface with denatured or isopropyl alcohol and avoid touching it.

Oil Sealer

Oil sealers adhere well to the surface of metal and provide a barrier to help protect it from moisture and prevent rust. Some metal artists use organic oils such as olive oil, linseed oil and nut oils to seal their steel work. In my view, organic oils tend to break down over time and do not offer the level of protection that synthetic oils provide.

Most synthetic metal oils are petroleum based and some also contain rust inhibitors and UV protection as an added plus. I often apply oil as a first sealer coat because it is extremely effective at preventing rust, particularly on pieces with a lot of detail or layers.

I have successfully used two brands of oil sealer available in the U.S.: Metal Oil® from Sculpt Nouveau and Flood Penetrol Oil Based Paint Additive® available from Amazon and various paint suppliers. Both are effective.

Safety alert: Synthetic oil sealers are petroleum based and should be handled with caution. Wear protective gloves as well as eye or face protection. Keep away from heat. Use outdoors or in a well-ventilated area. Do not breathe the vapor.

---

1 **Apply oil.** To apply the oil, I use a wool dauber with a thin wire handle that is often used for dyeing leather. Dip the dauber into the oil, then use a paper towel to wring out excess oil. The key is to apply a very, very thin coat of oil across the surface. If the oil is applied too thickly, it will remain tacky rather than dry. Be sure to push the oil into any crevices and tight spots of joins.

2 **Rub with steel wool.** After you apply the oil, use a small piece of fine steel wool to gently rub the oil into the surface. This step helps ensure thorough coverage.

3 **Wipe with paper towel**. Using a paper towel or rag, wipe the metal to remove any excess oil.

4 **Cure**. Finally, allow the oil to cure for three or four days. It will dry to a matte finish. If desired, a second thin coat of oil sealer can be applied as can a coat of wax or lacquer sealer, as described later in this chapter.

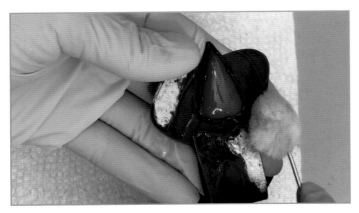

Step 1–Using a wool dauber, apply a very thin coat of oil to the metal.

Step 2–Using a small piece of steel wool, rub the oil into the metal surface.

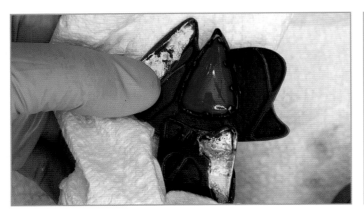

Step 3–Using a paper towel or rag, wipe off any excess oil.

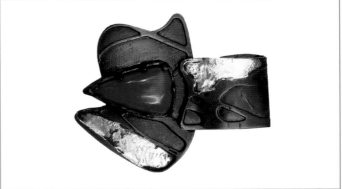

Step 4–Allow the oil sealer to cure for three or four days.

Wax Sealer

A wax finish will provide years of protection. In my experience, Renaissance Wax Polish®, the microcrystalline wax often used by many jewelers to protect silver and gold jewelry is not quite durable enough to adequately protect steel jewelry. Instead, I prefer a thicker wax containing hardeners. Waxes that contain UV inhibitors are also helpful to guard against corrosion. A wax sealer can be applied over oil or lacquer sealers for extra protection. However, these other sealers will not adhere to a waxed surface.

I have successfully used two brands of wax sealer available in the U.S.—Metal Wax® from Sculpt Nouveau and Bowling Alley Wax® manufactured by BWC Company and available from Amazon. Both contain carnauba wax, which is derived from the carnauba palm that grows only in Brazil. Carnauba wax is often used to make auto and floor waxes and, because of its hypoallergenic properties, is also found in many cosmetics. Any carnauba-based wax is likely to work just fine as a sealer for steel jewelry.

> **Safety alert**: Wax sealers contain solvents and should be handled with care. Avoid inhaling the fumes and wear protective gloves. Solvents are flammable and should be kept away from flame or extreme heat.

1 **Warm metal and apply wax**. Before applying wax, use a heat gun or hair dryer to warm the metal to about 150°F (66°C) to ensure that it is completely dry and to help the wax melt smoothly across the surface. The wax can be applied to cold metal, but warming it helps the wax cover evenly and reach into tight spaces. I use a cotton swab or cloth to apply the wax.

2 **Allow wax to dry**. Allow it to dry for about 5 to 10 minutes or until it is matte. Don't wait more than an hour or the wax will become too hard.

3 **Buff surface**. Buff it briskly with cheesecloth or a paper towel to remove any stickiness. Up to three coats of wax can be applied, but one or two are usually sufficient.

4 **Polish with cloth or brush**. After the final coat of wax, vigorously buff the surface using a soft cloth or a horsehair shoe brush. Wax sealers dry to a lovely satin finish that appears to have some visual depth.

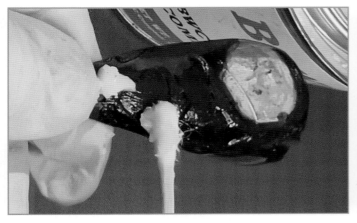

Step 1–After warming the metal, apply the wax using a cotton swab or cloth.

Step 2–In 5 to 10 minutes, the wax will dry to a dull matte finish.

Step 3–Using cheese cloth or a paper towel, buff the wax until it is no longer tacky.

Step 4–Using a horsehair shoe brush or soft cloth, polish the wax coating.

Lacquer Sealer

The third option, a lacquer sealer, is available either as water-based or solvent-based. In water-based sealers, polymer particles are dispersed into water and form an emulsion, meaning the particles are suspended rather than dissolved. In solvent-based sealers, the polymers are dissolved in a solvent such as tert-butyl acetate. Both types of sealers can provide good results; however, some artists feel that water-based coatings cause the jewelry to take on a plastic like appearance. I have found that solvent-based lacquers don't have this problem and provide attractive and durable protection.

 Safety alert: Solvent-based sealers emit strong smelling fumes and whenever possible should be used outdoors.

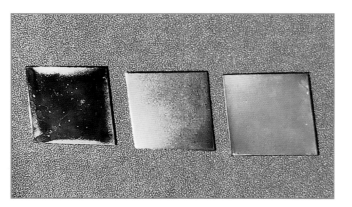
Lacquer sealers in gloss, satin and matte finishes.

One advantage of liquid coatings is that they come in a variety of finishes—gloss, satin and matte—allowing the artist to choose a finish that complements the aesthetics of the jewelry. Many outstanding lacquer sealers are available under a variety of brand names. Experiment with different ones and you'll soon develop a preference.

Lacquer sealers can be applied by spraying, dipping or brushing, ideally use them outdoors to avoid exposure to the fumes. Always wear a breathing mask and gloves. If spraying, use light even coats. If brushing, a cheap foam paintbrush works well to minimize brush marks. To dry the lacquer sealer, you may need to suspend the piece of jewelry to avoid marks occurring on the surface. I have found that a chopstick or thin dowel works well for this purpose. Simply weigh down one end of the chopstick or dowel on a table or bench and suspend the jewelry from the other end. If you cannot avoid marks during the drying process, these can be carefully touched up later. Lacquers usually dry to the touch after an hour or two and a second coat can be applied. A third coat can be applied, but sometimes results in a plastic-like finish.

The lacquer can be cured in a warm oven for a few hours, but it will also cure at room temperature over a few days.

Spray lacquer should be applied outdoors to avoid breathing the fumes.

An inexpensive foam brush is useful for applying lacquer.

Choosing the Right Sealer

Your choice of sealer(s) should be based on your aesthetic preference and the environment in which the jewelry will be worn. An oil sealer produces a matte finish, wax sealer produces a satin finish, and lacquer sealers are available in gloss, satin and matte finishes. Your design vision will dictate whether you want a glossy, semi-glossy or matte finish. I lean toward a matte finish because I want my work to appear somewhat weathered.

If a piece of steel jewelry will be worn in a harsh environment, particularly one that is humid, it is a good idea to apply two or three layers of sealers. All of the layers can be the same or you may combine different types of sealers. Keep in mind that if you use an oil sealer it should be applied as the first layer because it will not adhere to other sealers. Wax and lacquer sealers can be layered over oil, and wax can be layered over any other sealer. However, oil and lacquer cannot be applied over a wax sealer.

I often apply oil as the first sealer layer because it is very effective at preventing rust, particularly for more intricate or layered pieces. Jewelry that has intricate detail is more susceptible to crevice corrosion, which can occur when moisture becomes trapped in small pockets and cannot escape. Oil easily flows into these small spaces to help prevent crevice corrosion.

Applying an oil sealer as the first layer is effective for avoiding crevice corrosion in a piece of jewelry with significant detail.

Troubleshooting

- **Rust develops after the sealer is applied**. Rust can develop for several reasons. If the jewelry is not wiped with alcohol before applying a sealer, it is possible that oil or dirt on the metal surface has promoted rust. Also, if the sealer is not applied immediately after the patina, it is likely that rust will develop. Finally, if the sealer is not applied thoroughly across the entire surface, any unsealed areas are likely to rust. If rust develops, the sealer and patina should be removed by placing the jewelry in pickle and then scrubbing it clean. It may not be possible to remove the patina completely, but when you reapply the patina, it will mask any traces of the initial coat. Another more aggressive method to remove sealer and patina is to use a torch to burn them off, which will leave a heavy layer of oxidation, which will need to be removed by soaking the piece in pickle and scrubbing the metal with a stiff wire brush.

- **Lacquer sealer dries with a chalky film**. Occasionally a chalky film will develop on the surface of a lacquer sealer if it has been applied too heavily. If this occurs, simply apply another very thin layer of sealer and the chalky appearance will be resolved.

- **Oil sealer is sticky and won't dry**. Oil sealer must be applied in an extremely thin layer to avoid this problem. If it remains sticky, the sealer must be removed as described above and reapplied.

- **The sealer has left the jewelry with an odor**. Many sealers contain solvents that can cause the jewelry to have a chemical smell. The odor dissipates after a few days and is nothing to be concerned about.

Title: Cosmos Pendant
Artist: Bette Barnett
Description: Steel fused with bronzes and fine silver. 2024.

10. ENAMELLING ON STEEL
by Amanda Denison

When I considered including a chapter on enameling steel, I knew immediately that my choice for writing it would be Amanda Denison, who is recognized as one of the most distinctive jewelry enamelers in the world. Amanda works from her studio by the Thames in West London, an environment rich in inspiration with its overlapping natural/urban environment. Her work reflects this environment through the marks she makes in the enamel. Her work on steel has a haunting quality, reflecting traces of decay, dilapidation and dereliction.

Amanda graduated with an honors degree in Fine Arts and then went on to earn a BTEC diploma in Jewelry Making, receiving a double star distinction. In 2016 she was accepted to the Craft Council's renowned "*Hothouse Programme*", a British program of creative and business support for makers early in their careers. She was promoted by the Craft Council as "*One to Watch*", and was selected as a "*Rising Stars*" finalist in 2017. In 2016 she was accepted to the prestigious "*One Year On*" at New Designers, the longest running design showcase in England, sponsored by the Business Design Centre in Islington. Amanda's work has been exhibited throughout the UK, Europe and the USA and has been featured in journals and books on contemporary jewelery.

Website: amandadenison.com
Facebook: facebook.com/amandadenisonjewellery/
Instagram: @amandakdenison

ENAMELLING IS A PROCESS IN which glass particles are bonded onto metal at high temperature to form a layer of colour on the surface. Traditionally, **vitreous enamel** (fine ground glass) is applied in powder form to copper, silver and gold. When working on steel, however, I use **liquid enamel**. This is a mixture of enamel, water, clay and electrolytes.

There is a centuries old tradition of enamelling precious metals and copper, but it was not until the nineteenth century in Germany that enamel was first applied to sheet iron and steel. And, until recently, enamelled iron and steel were reserved for commercial enamelling applications such as signage, cookware, bathtubs and ovens. Today, enamel artists are exploring the rich opportunities that steel offers for experimenting with the enamelling process.

Steel is an affordable metal and it is fun to work with. It provides a great base on which to enamel and offers huge potential for experimentation. I love the freedom that working with steel and liquid enamel gives me to develop my own style and my own way of working. I originally studied fine art and this informs how I approach my work. I see the coated steel surface as a canvas on which to explore mark making. If you want a more intuitive and expressive way to enamel, using liquid enamel on steel will suit you. The best advice I can give you is to experiment, have fun and do not have fixed expectations. Be prepared to make mistakes; sometimes the most interesting effects are happy accidents.

Steels to Use for Enamelling

Various steels can be enamelled given the right preparation, including those listed here:

- **Pre-enamelled steel sheet**—steel sheet with a thin layer of enamel fired to each side available as whiteboard and chalkboard tiles.

- **Enamelling iron**—an ultra low-carbon steel alloy developed for enamelling.

- **Mild steel sheet**—low-carbon cold rolled steel, as described with greater detail in chapter 1, *Basics of Steel.* Cookware, such as pizza pans, is often made of mild steel and is easy to find and can be a cheap source of steel.

- **Stainless steel**—which contains chromium and is harder than mild steel, thus requiring roughening of the surface, as described later in this chapter.

- **Found steel**—miscellaneous items made of steel including spoons and ladles, food cans, nails, washers, wire and various panels of mesh and perforated steel.

Safety alert: A special warning regarding galvanized steel, which is steel that has been coated with a layer of zinc to protect it against rust and corrosion; when heated, galvanized steel gives off toxic fumes which can be fatal. It can only be used for enamelling once the coating has been sandblasted off. Galvanized steel is often lighter in colour and may have a frostier surface than other types of steel.

Pre-Enamelled Steel Sheet

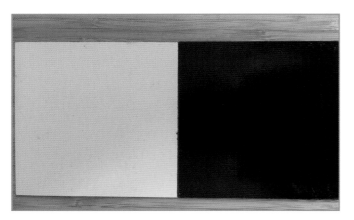

Pre-enamelled steel tile has a shiny white enamelled surface on one side and, on the other, a matte black one.

The pre-enamelled steel used in whiteboards is available in the U.S. as small steel tiles from Thompson Enamel and also Enamel Warehouse. These are my favourite steel surfaces for enamelling because most of the preparation needed for other forms of steel has been done and the pre-enamelled surface takes enamel beautifully. If you can get hold of some pre-enamelled steel, it is a great way to start enamelling on steel.

Pre-enamelled whiteboard steel is mild steel (usually 28-gauge) that has been enamelled on both sides. One side has a shiny white surface, the other side has a matte black surface. You can apply enamel to either surface.

To cut or drill pre-enamelled steel, *always* cover both sides of the sheet with masking tape to minimise splintering of the glass (enamel) surface. Cut using a jeweller's saw with saw blades designed for platinum in a 1/0 or 2/0 size or PepeTools Nano blades in a 2/0 size.*

*Jeweler saw blade sizes are numbered according to the cut, which refers to the teeth per inch. The numbering begins at #0 and the cuts become finer as the numbers increase with #8/0 being the finest. Conversely the numbers below #0 become coarser with #1, #2 and beyond for increasing coarseness.

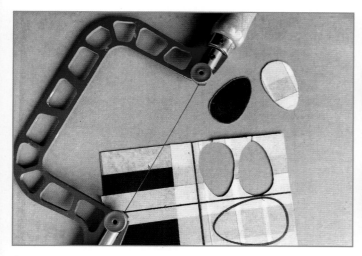

Pre-enamelled steel can be drilled or cut with a saw after covering the front and back with masking tape to prevent the enamel from breaking.

The tape should completely cover the back and front of the pre-enamelled steel before drilling or cutting it.

Alternatively, use heavy duty shears, aviation snips, or a guillotine or bench shear, or you can use an electric micro bandsaw. If you want to cut multiple shapes for, say, earrings, you may want to locate a waterjet cutting service. (Note that laser and plasma cutters cannot cut through the glass surface.)

Enamelling Iron

Enamelling iron is an ultra low-carbon steel alloy specifically developed for enamelling. It typically has carbon levels less than 0.05 percent and features a superior surface quality, which helps the enamel bond more effectively. In the U.S. enamelling iron is available from Thompson Enamel and Enamel Warehouse.*

Mild Steel

If you are buying steel sheet for enamelling, you should select low carbon mild steel, as described in detail in chapter 1. If you have a choice, use cold rolled mild steel rather than hot rolled, which often has mill scale (iron oxide) that forms on the surface during the hot-rolling process and can inhibit adhesion of enamel. In the USA, a grade 1008 is ideal, in the UK, BS CR4.** If you want to enamel on a contoured surface, mild steel can be formed before applying the enamel using either traditional forming methods or a **hydraulic press**.

Higher carbon steel should be avoided because the higher carbon content can result in gas bubbles forming during firing. These cause poor adhesion and penetrate the enamel resulting in dots on the surface. If this happens you can rub these back and fire another coat of enamel over the top. I always accept the bubbles and incorporate them into my design, but they can be a problem.

The downside to mild steel is that it rusts easily. For many of you this can be a nuisance because when you apply liquid enamel to the surface of mild steel, it can start to rust and you must move forward quickly with the firing process, as described later in this chapter.

*As of this book's publication date, Kat Cole, a U.S. based enamel artist, offers enamelling iron for sale (https://kat-cole.com). Enamelling iron is not widely available outside the U.S.
**For more information on low carbon mild steel, including the grading system, refer to chapter 1.

Inexpensive pizza pans and oven trays, available where household goods are sold, are a popular source of steel and one of the cheapest ways to get smaller quantities of thin gauge mild steel sheet (around 24 gauge). Do not assume that your pan or tray is made from mild steel, however, as many cheap cookware items are aluminium, which has a low melting point and cannot be enamelled. Similarly, many food cans are plastic coated aluminium. I take a magnet with me to the store to test the metal. Iron is magnetic, aluminium is not, so any metal with iron in it, such as steel, will be attracted to a magnet. The magnet test for steel is not foolproof (some stainless steels are not magnetic), but it helps you to eliminate those items that are made from other metals.

> **Safety alert**: Pizza pan/oven tray steel usually comes with a non-stick anti-corrosive coating which you will need to remove completely, either by sandblasting or by sanding with a coarse sandpaper (60–80 grit) or a grinding wheel. It is essential that you wear a particulate mask and goggles whichever method you use.

You can add texture to your mild steel before you apply enamel. Mild steel can be etched (electro-etching is ideal) or textured with hammers and punches to make marks. Holes can be drilled into the surface. If you do this before you apply liquid enamel, you will need to clear out the holes with a needle, or a similar sharp object before firing. If you drill holes after you fire your enamel, make sure you apply masking tape to both sides of the piece to minimise splintering when you drill. Texture can also be pressed onto the metal using a rolling mill, or textured and formed in a hydraulic press prior to enamelling.

Found Steel Metal

You can have great fun working with and repurposing steel from found objects. I love to give new life to something that has been discarded. I have experimented with enamel on all sorts of items: spoons and ladles, food cans, nails and washers, steel and iron wire and various mesh and perforated steel panels. You do need to be careful and the first question to ask is, "*Is it steel?*" If you are not sure, test it with a magnet. If it is attracted to the magnet, it is probably steel. Not all food cans (tin cans) are steel, and some are coated aluminium which has a low melting point and cannot be enamelled.

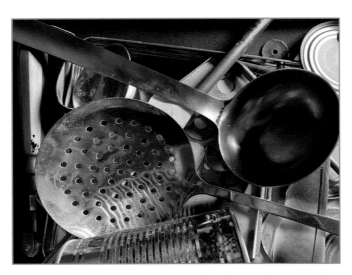

Other surfaces that appear to have an enamel coating may instead be powder coated, meaning the coating has been applied electrostatically as a powder and then cured under heat or an ultraviolet light, making it harder than conventional liquid paint. I suggest scratching with a pin or scissors to test. If the coating scratches easily it may be powder coated and should not be used.

You can have great fun repurposing found steel objects, such as spoons, ladles, nails and washers.

> **Safety alert**: Additionally, steel food cans may have an anti-corrosion plastic film on the inside, which you will need to burn off with a torch, working outdoors because of the toxic fumes released.

> **Safety alert**: Many steel found objects are galvanized, meaning they are coated with a layer of zinc to protect against rust and corrosion. Heating galvanized steel produces toxic fumes which can be lethal. Galvanised steel can be enamelled but only after you have totally removed the zinc coating by sandblasting with a coarse grit. For more information on galvanized steel, refer to chapter 1.

Stainless Steel

Stainless steel can be enamelled if it is prepared correctly by sandblasting. Stainless steel is tougher than other steels due to its chromium content. I have used a jeweller's saw to cut the handle off stainless steel spoons and to cut down kitchen implements. It's not difficult but it's slow work so take your time. Alternatively, you can use a cutting wheel on a Dremel, flex shaft or similar. Stainless steel sheet can be cut with a laser and plasma cutter.

Liquid Form Enamels

The process of bonding enamel to metal using heat is referred to as **fusion**. Enamel is available for application in powder (vitreous) or liquid form. Liquid enamel (also known as **porcelain enamel**, **industrial enamel** or **wet process enamel**) is the type of enamel most enamellers use with steel. It is a blend of enamel, water, clay and electrolytes and is available as a powder or pre-mixed as a liquid. It is always used in liquid form, hence its name, and if purchased in powder form, it must be mixed with water before applying it to the steel. I tend to buy it as pre-mixed liquid enamel, but this option is not available everywhere and delivery costs are invariably far higher than for powder. It is more likely that you will buy it as a powder and mix it yourself. There are many suppliers of liquid enamels, including Thompson Enamel, which sells products in the United States and Europe. The *Thompson Enamel Workbook*, available from the company's website (https://thompsonenamel.com), is a technical manual with a wealth of information about the Thompson range of enamels and enamelling processes.

I am based in the UK and use the English manufacturer W.G. Ball's Wet Process Enamels (their term for liquid enamels). Their enamels are also available in the U.S. The company's products include liquid opaque enamels in a wide range of colours. Although the website lists enamels separately for copper and steel, for the most part, they can be used interchangeably for either metal. The only exception is their **ground coats** where they produce one specifically for use with steel and another for use with copper. W.G. Ball's liquid enamels can also be mixed with Thompson Enamel's.

There are undoubtedly many other brands of liquid enamel that I am unaware of, so use whatever you can find, and experiment. Always take notes that you can refer to later. Unlike vitreous (powdered) enamels, liquid enamels can be mixed together like paints to create new colours.

Enamelling Process

In this section I will describe the basic steps involved in the enamelling process. Note that certain steps may not always be required, depending on the steel used and the desired effects.

Prepare the Steel

The bond between the initial layer of enamel and steel is crucial. Consequently, the preparation of the steel is of paramount importance if the enamel is to adhere well. Do not be tempted to rush or skip steps.

Nearly all types of steel used for enamelling must first be given some "tooth", meaning roughened to raise irregularities on the surface. The exception is pre-enamelled steel tiles that only need to be degreased before enamel is applied.

When you are working with enamel on steel, a sandblaster is your friend. Sandblasting is the most effective method to thoroughly prepare the surface of steel for enamelling. Use a medium-coarse sandblasting abrasive media, such as aluminum oxide, to give the surface some tooth so the enamel can grip. Many of us, myself included, do not have easy access to a sandblaster. There are alternatives available, although these are not quite as effective to add tooth to the surface. Thoroughly sand the steel with coarse sandpaper (60–80 grit) or use a grinding wheel to roughen the metal. After sandblasting, sanding or grinding, rinse the steel to remove any dust that remains on the surface.

The golden rule when enamelling is that your metal—in this case steel—always needs to be clean and free from grease. I degrease my metal by mixing pumice powder, available from jewellery supply vendors, with water to form a paste and then I scrub the metal using a brass brush. If you do not have pumice powder, use any gritty household cleaner. I finish off by using a Scotch-Brite® green scouring pad to further roughen the surface. Finally, hold the cleaned steel under the tap until the water runs off freely in a sheet rather than forming droplets that catch in the places where grease lingers. The best way for a final de-grease is to dip your finger into some wet liquid enamel and to rub it over the surface of the steel and then rinse. Quick and easy.

After degreasing, dry the steel with a paper towel but avoid touching the metal. Hold it at the sides; oil from fingerprints will prevent enamel from bonding to the steel.

Steel that is rusted or dirty (as shown on the left) will not be successful for enamelling. The steel needs to be cleaned thoroughly and abraded (as shown on the right).

Prepare the Enamel

If you are starting with unmixed liquid enamel in powder form, you will need to mix it with water to the proper consistency. Place some powder in a bowl and make a well in the centre. The amount of powder that is needed will depend on the size of the piece and the number of pieces that you are firing. After working with enamels for a while you will be able to easily estimate the amount needed.

Add water to the powder, a little at a time; tap water is fine. Let the water soak in and be absorbed into the powder before adding more. I add no more than a teaspoon of water at a time as I do not want it runny. As it gets wetter, stir to remove any lumps. If you intend to apply the liquid enamel by brushing, dipping or pouring it onto the steel surface, you are aiming for the consistency of pouring cream, slightly thicker than milk. If you plan to spray it onto the steel, you will want it slightly thinner. I never measure powder and water exactly. Instead, I add water until I am happy with the consistency. Many people like to test the thickness by dipping a spoon into the enamel or by dipping a finger in up to the first knuckle. Once the excess has flowed off, count the number of drops that fall. Three drops are ideal; less than three means the mixture is too thick. When it is the right consistency push it through a kitchen food sieve to remove any lumps.

To mix the enamel, place it in a bowl then make a well in the center of the powder.

Add water, a little at a time, and stir.

The mixed enamel should be the consistency of pouring cream, unless you plan to spray it, in which case, it should be a bit thinner.

When it is the right consistency, push it through a kitchen food sieve to remove any lumps.

If you are using pre-mixed liquid enamel, it needs to be shaken vigorously in its container for several minutes to mix it up and break up lumps. Add a little water if required and stir. When it is the right consistency push it through a sieve, into a bowl, as described previously.

Throughout your enamelling session you will need to stir your liquid enamel occasionally, as it will thicken quite quickly. Keep it covered with a lid or plastic film and, periodically, every three hours or so, push it through a sieve and add water as required.

Any unused mixed enamel can be stored in an airtight wide-necked jar. The liquid will evaporate and thicken over time so you will need to add more water and sieve it again before using. If it dries out and solidifies on the bottom of the jar, add a little hot water and let it soak in. If necessary, grind the lumps with a pestle and mortar (wear a mask when doing so) and then add water. Shake, stir and strain as before.

Apply a Ground Coat

An initial ground coat, also called a **grip coat**, needs to be applied first to nearly all steels before opaque liquid enamel can be added. Ground coat is a liquid enamel undercoat that contains metal oxides to promote bonding to steel and to enamels. Do not be tempted to apply a thick coat; a thin even coat of ground coat is required. In my experience a ground coat is usually needed for any steel that has not been sandblasted. The exception is pre-enamelled tiles which already have a ground coat applied.

If you have used a sandblaster to roughen the steel, you may be able to get away without using a ground coat, but there is no guarantee. If you have used sandpaper or a grinding wheel to roughen the surface, you should always use a ground coat. Ground coat is mixed in the same way as other liquid enamels—by adding water to the powder.

When you purchase a ground coat from an enamel supplier, make sure you use one specifically for steel. Although many liquid enamels can be used for both steel and copper, this does not apply to the ground coat. When fired, ground coat will bond with the steel to form either a dark grey/black or lighter grey layer, depending on which ground coat you purchase. The following table shows a selection of ground coats available from three different enamel suppliers and their colours after firing.

SELECTED GROUND COATS FOR STEEL		
Enamel Supplier	**Colour after Firing**	**Ground Coats**
W.G. Ball	Dark grey to black	Wet Process Enamel (Powder). Sheet Steel Ground coat 12559 (Liquid). Sheet Steel Ground coat 10543.
Enamel Warehouse	Dark grey to black	RM 27 Metal Frit Ground Coat for Steel.
Thompson Enamel	Light grey	GC16 Ground Coat for Steel Cobalt Blue (fires grey) Dry Powder.

I prefer a dark grey ground coat as I use a **sgraffito** technique, whereby I scratch through a layer of white enamel to reveal the dark ground coat layer below. I like the greater contrast achieved with a dark ground coat and white liquid enamel, but you may prefer a lighter grey ground coat if you are applying coloured liquid enamels rather than white. The sgraffito technique is described later in this chapter.

Steel tiles with ground coat that is (left to right) wet after application, dry and ready for firing, and fired.

Counter-Enamel if Needed

Counter-enamel is a coat of enamel applied to the reverse side of the metal to prevent it from warping during the firing process. Enamel expands and contracts at a different rate than metal during the heating and cooling processes and if the metal warps the enamel will crack or chip off immediately, or it may flake off later.

Warping is more likely to occur if you are enamelling thin steel (22-gauge/0.8 mm or thinner) and/or you are applying several coats of enamel. I also counter-enamel most pieces that are larger than four inches (100 mm) square. I use thin gauge steel wherever possible (26 to 22-gauge/0.4 mm to 0.8 mm) and usually only fire a single coat of enamel, so I rarely need to apply a counter coat to prevent warping. Although counter-enamelling is not always necessary it can be aesthetically desirable if you want an enamelled finish on the back, which is especially true when making earrings. You do not need to counter-enamel pre-enamelled steel as it is already enamelled on both sides.

To apply counter-enamel, I dip the steel into the liquid enamel so that both back and front surfaces are coated with enamel and both sides are then fired simultaneously. Ground coat and/or any liquid enamel can be used as a counter-enamel. You may choose to use different coloured enamels on the back and front surfaces. Once you have fired on a ground coat, rinse your piece and scrub it with a brass brush before applying a layer of liquid enamel.

Apply Liquid Enamels

Once a layer of liquid enamel ground coat has been fired onto the steel, you can then use all other liquid enamels and/or sift vitreous enamels (powdered jewellery enamel) over the liquid enamel ground coat. However, I always fire a layer of (white) liquid enamel before using vitreous enamel as it creates a good base for the vitreous enamel to adhere to.

Liquid enamel can be applied by brushing, painting, pouring, dipping or spraying it onto the steel. Whenever you apply liquid enamel, you are aiming for a thin even coat. A thick coat will crack or chip off during firing or subsequent stages. Keep it thin. I always work with white enamel, but you can use other colours. Once the surface of the steel has been coated with liquid enamel, tilt, tap and rotate the steel to allow any excess enamel to run off.

I like to apply the liquid enamel with a soft, wide paintbrush. A housepainter's brush is ideal for larger pieces where you want to cover the surface in one or two brush strokes. To pour the enamel on, use a spoon or a small jug to pour the liquid enamel onto the steel. Gently tilt and rotate the metal until it has a thin, even coat of enamel. If you wish, you can dip the steel into the liquid enamel. Hold the steel with your fingers or plastic tongs and gently dip it into the liquid enamel, tilt and rotate it so the enamel spreads evenly across both the front and back surfaces.

Liquid enamel can be applied by brushing with a soft, wide paintbrush.

Another method is to apply liquid enamel by pouring it onto the surface of the steel.

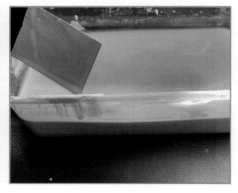
Dipping the steel into the liquid form enamel while holding it with your fingers or plastic tongs is another method of application.

Safety alert: Spraying the enamel will give you a lovely thin even coat. It can be done with a spray gun and compressor or with a can of air propellant and spray attachment. You need a well-ventilated spray booth of some sort and must wear a mask and goggles. Although I would love to be able to spray my enamels, I work from a tiny studio and it is not possible. The process of spraying enamels has been refined by enamel artist John Killmaster whose "granular spray" technique builds up thin layers of enamel to enable fine sgraffito techniques.[17]

Dry the Enamel

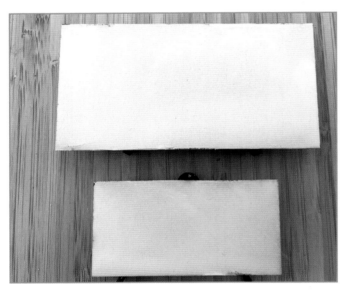

After drying the enamel, it is ready for firing or the sgraffito technique, as described in the following section.

It is essential that the liquid enamel has dried completely before you move any further. You can place the coated steel on a trivet on top of a preheated kiln and allow it to dry or use a heat gun or hairdryer (wear a mask). When the enamel dries it forms a pale, chalky coating on the surface of the steel.

Rusting is an issue with mild steel and the minute liquid of any sort is applied, it can start to rust, so you want it to dry quickly. Rusting is not an issue if you have applied a ground coat, or with stainless steel or pre-enamelled steel. When using these metals I often apply enamel to multiple pieces and place them on sheets of paper to dry overnight.

Once dry you will need to clean the back of the piece with a slightly dampened cloth to remove any unwanted drips or splashes of liquid enamel.

Sgraffito Technique, if Desired

This is where the fun and exploration start. Sgraffito is a mark making technique where lines or marks are drawn into the dry unfired enamel, exposing the layer underneath, whether this be bare metal, ground coat, or a previously enamelled layer. Traditionally done with powdered vitreous enamel, sgraffito is a wonderful technique to use with liquid enamel and fine detail can be achieved. I like to make abstract marks, but you can also work figuratively. Both work well.

The dried enamel forms a chalky coating on the metal. Many different types of tools can be used for making marks in the surface. Sharp sticks, scribes, needles and steel burnishers work well. I am always on the lookout for items to add to my collection of sgraffito drawing tools. Over the years I have amassed quite a few. Some are natural materials, such as sticks that I sharpen to use, thorns, dried teasel heads, pine needles, pieces of bamboo and porcupine quills. Others are drawing instruments and household objects: traditional ink pen nibs, automatic pencils, scalpel blades and craft knives. I have a fine stash of needles in different thicknesses, and different sized combs and wheels (butter wheels, dressmaking wheels and even wheels from LEGO® models) to push across the surface. I lay down stencils and draw through them or use perforated card or metal to mark circles at regular intervals. It is fun to experiment and see what makes the most interesting marks.

A collection of sgraffito drawing tools, including ink pen nibs, automatic pencils, a nit comb and craft knives.

Natural sgraffito mark making tools including sharpened sticks, thorns, dried teasel heads, pine needles, feathers, and porcupine quills

As you create marks in the enamel, tap your piece periodically so that any enamel trapped in your marks falls free. Otherwise, you will find your marks are blurred and indistinct when they fire. I also use a very soft brush (I prefer fan shaped artist brushes) to gently brush along all the marks and remove any last bits of powder. This will make your image more refined and bolder. If you brush the excess off onto a clean piece of paper, you can return all the enamel dust to your liquid enamel container so you do not waste it.

Safety alert: Again, remember to always wear a mask whenever you are working with dry enamel.

As you make marks, excess dry enamel will collect, which can result in blurred marks unless tapped or brushed off.

After tapping or brushing off the excess powder, the marks are sharper and will be much more distinct when fired.

Here is an example of some sgrafitto marks after firing.

Another example, showing the wide variety of marks that can be achieved.

Fire Enamels

When enamels are heated to high temperatures, they fuse to the metal or previous layer of fused enamel. The temperature at which the glass fuses is referred to as the **firing temperature**. The heat source for firing enamels can be either a kiln or a gas torch. In either case you will be working with very high temperatures. Before firing you will need to place your piece on a trivet, firing rack or other support device. Trivets come in different shapes and sizes and are made of titanium or steel. Select the support/base that is most appropriate for the size and shape of your pieces.

 Safety alert: When firing enamels, whether you use a kiln or a torch, you are working with very high temperatures. Wear heat resistant gloves to protect your hands and safety glasses to protect your eyes.

Be aware that if your piece is counter-enamelled, you risk depositing enamel on the trivet during the firing process. I minimise the likelihood of this happening by using kiln wash, also called shelf wash, which is available from pottery suppliers. I just mix it with water and paint it onto the trivet prongs. Alternatively, I rub chalk over the prongs to protect them.

Every time you add a new layer of enamel and fire it, there are gains and losses. With each layer, you can add more colour, but you will get some deterioration to lines or surface quality. It is a balancing act. For enamelling iron, mild steel and found steel, you can fire two or three times maximum in addition to a ground coat. For stainless steel, the maximum is four to five times. Play about with it, see what happens and what works for you.

Kiln Firing. A kiln is an oven or furnace that provides high consistent heat. Kilns are commonly used to fire ceramics but also used for enamelling. The kiln is effectively a chamber where the hot air surrounds the enamel coated metal and heats both enamel and metal simultaneously. Most enamellers use electric front opening kilns specifically designed for enamelling.

When working with a kiln, make sure you have enough space around it to work safely. I have my kiln sitting on a fire-proof surface and surround it with ceramic tiles. This provides a safe surface on which to place hot items to cool when they come out of the kiln and is a safety measure in case I drop hot items when I remove them from the kiln.

Preheat your kiln to the desired firing temperature. In general steel fires at 1470° to 1510°F (800° to 820°C) compared to copper and silver, which fire at 1450° to 1500°F (788° to 816°C). However, each kiln is different and firing times and temperatures will vary slightly. When firing enamel on steel, I set my kiln for 1470°F (800°C).

After placing your piece on a trivet, use a firing fork to move it in and out of the kiln. A firing fork is a long-handled fork that is designed to support the enamelling trivet as you place it into and remove it from the kiln.

Each time you open the kiln door the temperature drops and you must wait until it rises back up to the set temperature, in this case 1470°F (800°C). Once the kiln reaches that temperature, I usually fire the piece for around two minutes before removing it from the kiln.

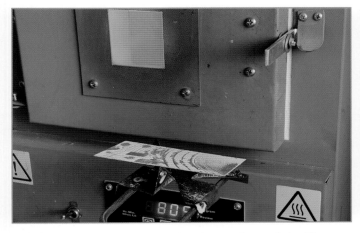

Use a firing fork to move your piece into and out of the kiln.

Each time you open the kiln door the temperature drops and must rise back up to the set temperature at which point you begin timing the firing period.

Remove the piece from the kiln using the firing fork and check to see that the enamel is smooth and shiny. If it's bumpy and not quite ready, pop it back in for a little longer. After firing, allow your piece to air cool for a minute before you dip it in water.

Be aware that if you have had your kiln on for a few hours there will be residual heat that builds up and firing times will be shorter.

Torch Firing. You can successfully use a gas torch to fire enamel on steel. When I first started to enamel, I torch fired as I did not have access to a kiln. With torch firing the torch heats the metal from below and the metal, in turn, melts the enamel. One disadvantage of torch firing is that it can be difficult to heat the steel evenly, particularly with larger pieces because steel is a poor conductor of heat. On the plus side, however, using a torch allows you to watch what happens as the enamel reacts to the heat, and it is easier to gauge firing times.

You will need a torch that produces sufficient heat. Smaller micro-torches are not hot enough. The gas you use will also have a bearing on the amount of heat generated. Torches that are fuelled with propane, MAPP and acetylene can be used. A torch and gas bottle from the hardware store is fine; a Sievert Torch or Smith Little Torch is better.

To torch fire a smaller piece, I place it on a titanium or steel trivet. Then I place the trivet on a steel screen that is supported atop a tripod. Using a hot flame, heat the steel from underneath and keep the flame moving to heat the entire surface. Stop heating when the surface of the enamel is smooth and even. Allow it to air cool for a couple of minutes before you rinse it in water.

It's easier to heat the steel evenly when working with smaller pieces. For larger pieces, I use fire bricks to build a temporary open fronted box structure to help trap the heat and keep it from dissipating. Another way to trap the heat is to use a large steel can. The internet is a great resource for ideas on how to do this, but make sure you have a safe area and enough space in which to work safely.

 Safety alert: When using a torch for enamel firing, you will need a hot flame. To protect your eyes from ultraviolet and infrared light waves, wear protective tinted glasses. There is some evidence that cataracts can form if eyes are unprotected from the light.

You can successfully torch fire the enamel by heating the metal from below and allowing the metal in turn to melt the enamel.

Abrade the Surface

After firing, the enamel will be shiny and glassy, and the sgraffito marks will be quite crude. There are many reasons why you may wish to abrade or stone back the surface. The obvious one is to even out any lumps or bumps, especially if you wish to fire on another layer of enamel. You may also prefer to create a matte surface rather than the high gloss enamelled surface. I abrade the surface to create a matte finish and to soften the sgraffito marks that I have made. Gently abrading or rubbing the surface softens and refines the marks. Over time you will learn how much pressure to apply and the effects you can achieve. If you are using pre-enamelled steel or have first fired a ground coat, abrading reveals the darker layer below and creates subtle areas of hue and tone. You can also stone back to the bare steel if you want some contrast or, like me, if you would like your pieces to rust in certain areas.

 Safety alert: Abrading the surface of enamel releases small particles into the air. Be sure to wear a particulate mask to protect your lungs.

Lumps and bumps are common in fired enamel and you may want to abrade them to create a smoother surface.

The abraded surface is smooth with a matte finish.

So how do you go about abrading the surface? There are several materials you can use for this, and they should all be used with water. You can gently grind the surface using a stone under running water or by wetting the surface of the enamel and dipping it regularly into a bowl of water. The traditional stones to use are carborundum stones made from silicon carbide, or alundum stones, made from white aluminium oxide. Both can leave scratches on the surface, but alundum stones are less harsh and available in different grits. Silicon carbide sanding papers used wet will also work but using them is a slow and laborious process.

I prefer to use a diamond pad, which is used in glass studios and auto repair shops. These sponge pads are backed with a fabric embedded with diamond abrasive material. The diamond fabric comes in several forms: sponge sanding pads, strips of fabric or flex shaft (pendant drill) attachments. The sponge pads and the fabric come in different grits and I tend to use a medium grit and a fine grit. I avoid the super coarse grit which leaves scratch marks, or the finest grit which is not very effective. The strips of fabric can be wrapped around sticks or shaped with your fingers and worked into tight areas. Make sure you use them with water.

Diamond pads in various forms, such as sponge sanding pads and strips of fabric, are effective materials for abrading the enamel.

If you want simply to create a matte surface finish and do not want to take the time to abrade the surface, you can use matting salts in solution or etching cream. Etching cream is typically made from hydrofluoric or sulfuric acid and is available from Thompson Enamel as ETCH-4 Etchall® Etching Cream.

Safety alert: Be aware that these solutions are harsh and toxic so be sure to follow the safety instructions from the manufacturer.

Seal the Surface

When I have abraded the enamel and I am happy with it, I seal it with a coating of wax. I like to use Renaissance Wax®, a microcrystalline wax polish developed by the British Museum in London as a conservation wax. It is commonly used to polish and conserve metal and is used on gemstones and organic materials such as wood and tortoiseshell. To use Renaissance Wax®, put a tiny amount of it on a cotton cloth and rub over the surface. Leave for a few seconds then buff. The wax will deepen the colour of the enamel, enhance the marks made and preserve the surface. Any carnauba wax will also work but tends to mute the colour. Alternatively, you can use a matte lacquer spray sealant, although I find this results in a satin sheen rather than a matte finish.

Other Techniques to Try

After you have fired your ground coat or your first coat of liquid enamel you can move on to exploring other things in addition to sgraffito techniques. A ground coat will bond with liquid enamels or vitreous enamels (powdered jewellery enamel) and you can now build up areas of different colours.

Add Texture

You can draw or stamp images on the surface (using water soluble inks) and sift on and fire vitreous enamel. Or you can roughen the surface slightly and then draw with a graphite pencil or use wax crayons specially made for enamelling. You can paint with underglaze for a matte finish or overglaze (also known as onglaze) and watercolour enamels for a shiny finish. You can screen print onto the surface or use decals and you can add metallic foils to the surface. Texture can be added by mixing sand or fire scale (copper oxide) with liquid (or vitreous) enamels and firing. In fact, the possibilities are endless.

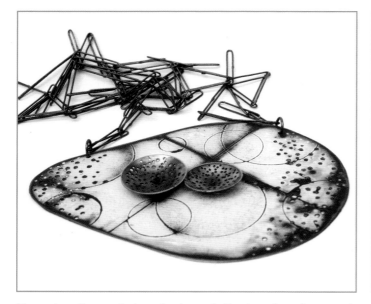
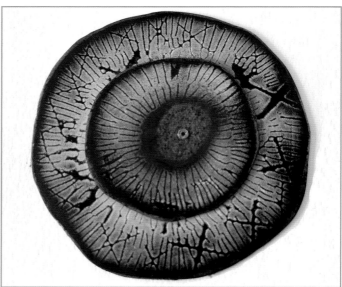

Examples of enamel pieces by Amanda Denison featuring rusted surface treatments.

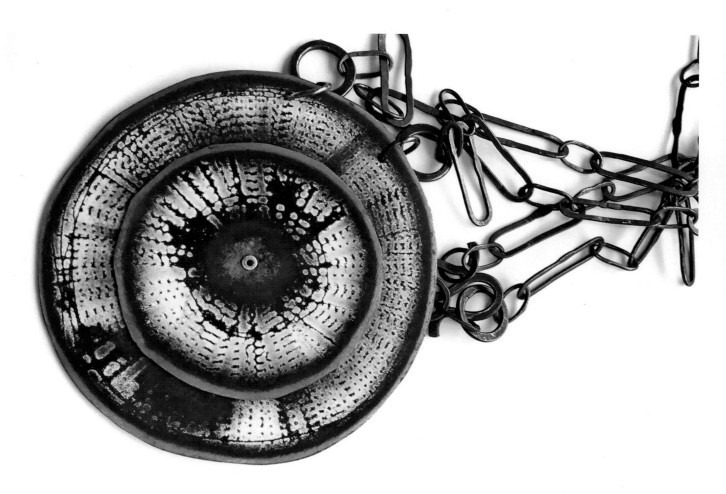

Enamel piece by Amanda Denison featuring rusted surface treatment.

Health and Safety

• You should invest in the following protective items: heat proof gloves, mask, clear goggles and protective safety glasses.

• Do not have any food or drink in the studio when you work with any sort of enamel.

• If you are hand cutting steel always wear goggles, a mask and gloves (I wear soft gardening gloves with a leather palm and finger pads).

• Always wear a particulate mask when working with dry liquid enamel powder. It's much finer than vitreous enamel and you don't want to inhale it.

• When cleaning up use a damp sponge to wipe surfaces. Never sweep up enamel from the floor (enamel particles will be stirred up and rise so you will inhale them). Instead, use a spray bottle filled with water and spray water into the air, which encourages the enamel particles to drop and settle on the floor. Leave overnight and in the morning, use a mop or vacuum cleaner to clean the floor.

Information on Different Types of Steel

PRE-ENAMELLED STEEL	Preparation	No sandblasting or sanding required. Degrease thoroughly.
	Ground coat	Ground coat is not required.
	Applying enamel	Brushing, dipping, pouring, spraying.
	Number of firings possible	2 to 3.
	Cutting by hand	Always wear goggles and gloves to protect from steel splinters. Apply masking tape on both sides. Cut using: jeweller's saw and Nano blades / platinum blades, aviation snips, guillotine, or bench shear. Can also use a micro band saw.
	Cutting multiple shapes from large sheets of steel	Water-jet cutter (laser and plasma cutters cannot be used).
	Can this steel rust?	Yes, but only when bare steel is exposed.
ENAMELLING IRON	Preparation	Sandblasting preferrable (if not, sand with a coarse sanding paper 60/80 grit). De-grease thoroughly.
	Ground coat	Ground coat is not required if sandblasted (otherwise it may be required).
	Applying enamel	Brushing, dipping, pouring, spraying.
	Number of firings possible	Several.
	Cutting by hand	Always wear goggles and gloves to protect from steel splinters. Apply masking tape on both sides along cutting lines. Cut using: jeweller's saw and Nano blades / platinum blades, aviation snips, guillotine, or bench shear. Can also use a micro band saw.
	Cutting multiple shapes from large sheets of steel	Not applicable (sold in small sheets or shapes).
	Can this steel rust?	Yes, when bare steel is exposed.
	Forming	Can be bent/folded and can be formed using doming blocks and punches or by using a hammer and silversmithing stakes. Thinner gauge steel can be formed with a hydraulic press.

LOW CARBON MILD STEEL	Preparation	Sandblasting preferrable (or sand with a coarse sanding paper 60/80 grit, or use a bench grinder). De-grease thoroughly.
	Ground coat	Yes.
	Applying enamel	Brushing, dipping, pouring, spraying.
	Number of firings possible	2 to 3.
	Cutting by hand	Always wear goggles and gloves to protect from steel splinters. Thin gauge steel up to about 20 ga./0.9 mm can be cut with a jeweller's saw and Nano blades / platinum blades, aviation snips, guillotine, or bench shear. You can use pancake dies or a disc cutter in a hydraulic press to a maximum of 18 ga./1.2 mm max. Can also use a micro band saw.
	Cutting multiple shapes from large sheets of steel	Laser cut.
	Can this steel rust?	Yes, mild steel rusts easily when exposed to air or liquid.
	Forming	Can be bent/folded and can be formed using doming blocks and punches or by using hammer and silversmithing stakes. Thinner gauge steel can be formed with a hydraulic press.
STAINLESS STEEL	Preparation	Sandblasting preferrable (or sand with a coarse sanding paper 60/80 grit). De-grease thoroughly.
	Ground coat	Ground coat usually required.
	Applying enamel	Brushing, dipping, pouring, spraying.
	Number of firings possible	Several (4 to 5).
	Cutting by hand	Always wear goggles and gloves to protect from steel splinters (tougher than mild steel and harder to cut). Cut using: jeweller's saw and Nano blades / platinum blades. Can also use a micro band saw or a cutting blade with a Dremel.
	Cutting multiple shapes from large sheets of steel	Laser cut.
	Can this steel rust?	No.

PIZZA PAN/OVEN TRAY STEEL Test with magnet	Preparation	Sandblasting preferrable (or sand with a coarse sanding paper 60/80 grit or use a bench grinder). De-grease thoroughly.
	Ground coat	Yes.
	Applying enamel	Brushing, dipping, pouring, spraying.
	Number of firings possible	2 to 3.
	Cutting by hand	Depends on steel and gauge. Always wear goggles and gloves to protect from steel splinters. Thin gauge steel up to about 20 ga/0.9 mm can be cut with a jeweller's saw and Nano blades / platinum blades, aviation snips, guillotine, or bench shear. You can use pancake dies or a disc cutter in a hydraulic press to a maximum of 18 ga./1.2 mm max.
	Cutting multiple shapes from large sheets of steel	Not applicable.
	Can this steel rust?	Yes.
	Forming	Can be formed using doming blocks and punches or by using a hammer and silversmithing stakes. Can be formed with a hydraulic press.
FOUND STEEL (FOOD CANS, FOUND SHEET) Test with magnet	Preparation	Sandblasting. De-grease thoroughly.
	Ground coat	Ground coat required.
	Applying enamel	Brushing, dipping, pouring, spraying.
	Number of firings possible	2 to 3.
	Cutting by hand	Always wear goggles and gloves to protect from steel splinters. Cut using: jeweller's saw and Nano blades / platinum blades. Can also use a micro band saw.
	Cutting multiple shapes from large sheets of steel	Laser.
	Can this steel rust?	It depends on the composition of the steel, but it can often rust.

11. GALLERY

Title: Fine Art Necklace
Artist: Mike Edelman
Description: Necklace of steel, bronze and copper. About 9 in. x 3 in. x 1 in. 2023.

Title: Pile in Red
Artist: Kat Cole
Description: Pendant of steel and vitreous enamel. Hollow fabricated, soldered, kiln-fired liquid-form enamel. 2017.

Title: Sea Breeze in Steel
Artist: Julie Billups
Description: Pendant constructed with sintered steel tiles. Surfaces are either layered vitreous enamel or 24k gold Keum Boo. 2023.

Title: Paperchain Collar
Artist: Susanne Henry
Description: Necklace of mild steel. 2018.
Photographer: Jocelyn Negron.

Title: Traces
Artist: Amanda Denison
Description: Brooch of enamel on mild steel with hand drawn marks, abraded and rusted after firing. 3 tiers, riveted. 64 mm/2-1/2 in. 2022.

Title: Meeting Necklace II
Artist: Deborah Vivas and Melissa Smith
Description: Necklace of mild steel, 24k gold, .999 silver and .925 silver. Fabricated, fused, scored, formed, textured, burnished, heat patina. 2022.

Title: Wave
Artist: Gail Golden
Description: Cuff of etched mild steel fused with 18k gold, white diamonds. Nail polish used as etching resist. 2022.

Title: Piercinged Ring
Artist: János Gábor Varga
Description: Ring of iron and 18k gold. Forged iron and soldered gold. 2021.

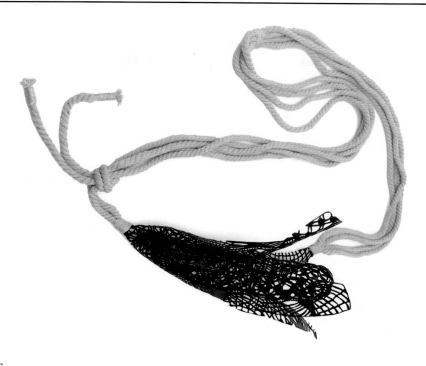

Title: Banana Necklace
Artist: April Wood
Description: Necklace of steel, dyed cotton cord, embroidery thread. 2021.

Title: Beauty from Ashes
Artist: Hengamesh Kashani
Description: Earrings with gold leaf sgraffito on pre-enameled steel (blackboard). 2020.

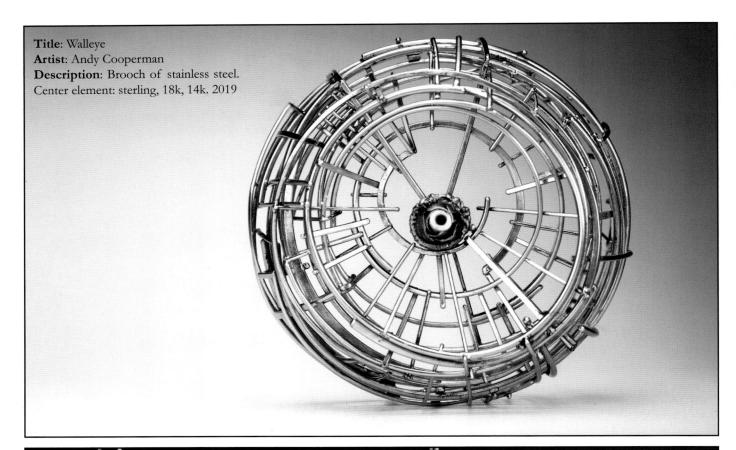

Title: Walleye
Artist: Andy Cooperman
Description: Brooch of stainless steel.
Center element: sterling, 18k, 14k. 2019

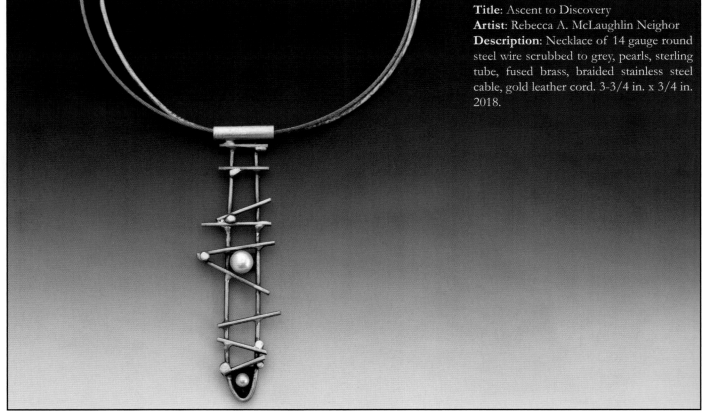

Title: Ascent to Discovery
Artist: Rebecca A. McLaughlin Neighor
Description: Necklace of 14 gauge round
steel wire scrubbed to grey, pearls, sterling
tube, fused brass, braided stainless steel
cable, gold leather cord. 3-3/4 in. x 3/4 in.
2018.

Title: Oh What a Night!
Artist: Diana Hirschon
Description: Earrings of etched steel and sterling silver with 24K gold applied in Keum Boo process. 2022.

Title: Brooch
Artist: Pat Flynn
Description: Brooch of iron, 22k yellow gold, 18k white gold, diamonds. Scored and bent, fused, fabricated, stone setting. 1-1/2 in. x 2 in. x 1/4. in. 2013.
Photo: Hap Sakwa.
Collection: Private.

Title: Mine Forever
Artist: Kenneth McBain
Description: Ring made by lathe turning construction, stone setting. 2021.

Title: Oracle Pendant
Artist: Bette Barnett
Description: Steel pendant fused with 18k yellow gold, suspended from a hammered steel neck ring heavily fused with 18k gold. Prong set druzy chrysocolla. 2023.

ABOUT THE AUTHOR

Bette Barnett is a recognized authority on steel jewelry, a sought-after teacher and innovator in metalsmithing. In this landmark book, Bette shares her deep experience in a broad range of techniques for creating dramatic steel jewelry.

Bette began her metalsmithing career in 2010, and in 2013 the late Chris Nelson introduced her to steel and gold, engendering her ongoing passion for creating steel jewelry. Bette built on those studies by exploring, testing and perfecting techniques that had never been fully documented, including the ancient art of Keum Boo on steel, fusing alternative metals to steel, fusing powdered metals to steel and working with various non-traditional forms of steel such as perforated sheet and woven steel mesh.

As a leader in metals research, Bette has published articles on steel jewelry techniques in Lapidary Journal Jewelry Artist and MJSA Journal. She authored a research paper for the prestigious Santa Fe Symposium entitled "*Steel Jewelry-Expanding the Horizons of Steel and Gold*", which she presented to the Symposium in 2020. Bette's focus is on educating all metalsmiths—blacksmiths, bladesmiths and jewelers—encouraging them to step out of their comfort zones and explore the creative potential of steel jewelry.

Webpage: studiomigoto.com
Facebook: facebook.com/studiomigoto/, facebook.com/groups/steeljewelry
Instagram: @bettebarnett

PHOTO CREDITS

Page 9, Hermatite, Michael812/Shutterstock.com.

Page 9, Limonite, Marcel Clemens/Shutterstock.com.

Page 10, Junkyard Steel, Daniel Jedzura/Shutterstock.com.

Page 11, Cold rolled low carbon steel, Teh_z1b/Shutterstock.com.

Page 11, Hot rolled low carbon steel, Kutcenko/Shutterstock.com.

Page 14, Sheet metal, Alexandru Rosu/Shutterstock.com.

Page 17, Berlin iron jewelry, Metrpolitan Museum of Art.

Page 17, Alexander Calder cuff, Wikimedia Commons/Sailko

Page 19, Rust, PalSand/Shutterstocl.com.

Page 21, Droplets of water, Suriyachan/Shutterstock.com.

Page 21, Guillotine shears, Photo courtesy of Durston Tools.

Page 22, Aviation snips, Donatas 1205/Shutterstock.com.

Page 22, Tin snips, Vadym Zaitsev/Shutterstock.com.

Page 23, Hand saw, ValentinaFedukina/Shutterstock.com.

Page 37, Orion Pulse Arc Welder, Courtesy of Sunstone engineering.

Page 42, Examples of laser printed images, Dubova/Shutterstock.com.

Page 42, Laser printed image of text, Kirill Gorshkov/Shutterstock.com.

Page 43, Laser printed transfer, Dubova/Shutterstock.com.

Page 46, Copper sulfate, Boonchok/Shutterstock.com.

Page 47, Copper nitrate, RHJPhotos/Shutterstock.com.

Page 77, Statue of Liberty, Alamy.com.

Page 80, Placer gold, Bjoern Wylezich/Shutterstock.com.

Page 103, Rusted surface, Robert D. Young/Shutterstock.com

ENDNOTES

1. Chris Nelson, "*Iron Mused/Gold Fused…The New Iron Age*", The Santa Fe Symposium on Jewelry Manufacturing Technology 2014, ed. E. Bell and J. Haldeman (Albuquerque Met-Chem Research, 2014).

2. Bette Barnett, "*Steel Jewelry—Expanding the Horizons of Steel with Gold*", The Santa Fe Symposium on Jewelry Manufacturing Technology 2022, ed. E. Bell, J. Haldeman, M. Carr and J. Cast (Met-Chem Research,2022). 1–46.

3. John Cogswell, *Creative Stonesetting* (Brynmorgen Press 2008) 193–194.

4. John Cogswell, *Creative Stonesetting* (Brynmorgen Press 2008) 194.

5. National Material Company, "*Steel and Recycling: Fun Facts*", https://www.nationalmaterial.com/steel-and-recycling-fun-facts, August 6, 2020 News Blog.

6. "*Steel: Ancient Steel*", Wikepedia https://en.wikipedia.org/wiki/Wootz_steel.

7. "*Iron Age*", Wikepedia, https://en.wikipedia.org/wiki/Iron_Age.

8. "*The Mohs Scale of Hardness for Metals: Why It's Important*", Jewelry Notes, https://www.jewelrynotes.com/the-mohs-scale-of-hardness-for-metals-why-it-is-important/.

9. Brenda Schweder, *Steel Wire Jewelry: Stylish Designs, Simple Techniques, Artful Inspiration*, 1st ed. (New York: Lark Crafts, 2008).

10. Dr. Christopher W. Corti, "*Basic Metallurgy of the Precious Metals: Part 1*", The Santa Fe Symposium on Jewelry Manufacturing Technology 2017, ed. Eddie Bell (Albuquerque: Met-Chem Research, 2017), 31.

11. Komelia Hongja Okim, *Korean Metal Art: Techniques, Inspiration, and Traditions* (Atglen, PA Schiffer Publishing, Ltd. 2019) 118.

12. Tim McCreight, *Metals Technic* (digital edition), Komelia Okim, "*Kum-boo 24k Overlay on Silver*", 2014, location 1555.

13. Charles Lewton-Brain, *Keum Boo: Hot Burnished Gold Foil* (http://brainpress.com 1987).

14. Charles Lewton-Brain, *Keum Boo: Hot Burnished Gold Foil* (http://brainpress.com 1987).

15. Charles Lewton-Brain, "*Gold Applications: Compositional Systems: Part One*", The Santa Fe Symposium on Jewelry Manufacturing Technology, ed. Eddie Bell (Albuquerque: Met-Chem Research, 2016) 322.

16. Celie Fago, *Keum Boo on Silver: Techniques for Applying 24k Gold to Silver*, (Bethel, VT Celie Fago 2008) 60.

17. https://www.ganoksin.com/article/john-killmaster-the-quickening/.

GLOSSARY

[Please note that the definitions in this glossary were written to describe the terms as used in this book. Some have broader definitions.]

A

AISI.   American Iron and Steel Institute, which establishes standards for steel use in North America. There is significant overlap with SAE.

Anneal.   Process in which metal is heated and slowly cooled to make it more workable, usually after work hardening.

ASTM.   American Society for Testing and Materials, a globally recognized organization that develops standards in safety, quality and content of materials, including steel. ASTM, uses codes that consist of a letter followed by a sequentially assigned number that refer to different categories of materials, products or processes. The codes for ferrous metals, including steel, begin with the letter A.

Aviation snip.   Hand shear that typically can cut up to 18 gauge cold rolled steel or 22 gauge stainless steel. Color coded handles are based on the direction of the desired cut: red for counterclockwise cuts, green for clockwise cuts and yellow for straight cuts.

B

Baling wire, bale wire.   Soft steel wire typically used in agriculture and industry for a wide range of uses. Originally designed to bind bales of hay or straw, thinner gauges can be used in the same way as binding wire.

Base metals.   Common metals that are not considered precious, including copper, iron, thallium, zinc, nickel, aluminum, and lead. The lower market value of jewelry made of base metals has been attributed to the fact that they more readily oxidize and corrode.

Bench shear.   Also known as a lever shear. This is a mounted shear with a mechanism to increase the mechanical cutting advantage. It is usually used for cutting rough shapes out of medium-sized pieces of sheet metal but cannot do delicate work.

Bi-metallic corrosion.   See galvanic corrosion.

Binding wire.   Iron or stainless steel wire, usually thinner than 0.55 mm used as an aid in the soldering and brazing processes to secure or support metal being joined. Also used to wrap the edges of charcoal blocks to reduce cracking.

C

Capillary effect.   In soldering or brazing, the force that pulls molten solder through the channel created by microscopic irregularities in the metals.

Carbon steel, plain carbon steel.   Metal alloy combining iron and carbon plus other elements in smaller quantities including manganese, silicon and copper.

Carburize, carburization, carbonization. Process of increasing carbon content in the surface of steel by heating it in the presence of a carbon rich medium which weakens the metal and makes it more brittle.

Case hardening. See carburization, carbonization.

Cast iron. Class of iron-carbon alloys with a carbon content of more than 2 percent and silicon content of 1–3 percent. It has a relatively low melting temperature, making it castable.

Casting. Shaping a material, such as metal, by pouring it in its molten state into a mold and letting it harden without pressure.

Casting grains. Small grains or beads of metals. When alloying metals, the grains allow you to precisely measure the various components.

Coke. Solid black substance produced from coal by heating until the gas and tar are removed. To make steel in a blast furnace, coal must first be turned into coke, which when burned removes the oxygen from iron ore, leaving pure iron.

Cold rolled steel. Essentially hot rolled steel that is rolled a second time at room temperature, resulting in steel sheet that has a smoother finish, greater durability and tighter tolerances.

D

Damascus steel. Steel made with a wavy surface pattern produced by hammer-welding plates of steel and iron (and sometimes nickel) followed by repeated heating and forging, used chiefly for knife and sword blades.

Dross. Mass of solid impurities floating on or dispersed in a molten metal.

E

Electro-etching. Process where metal is etched by submerging it in an electrically conductive solution and applying electricity as direct current.

Electrolyte. In electro-etching, an electrically conductive chemical solution that causes metal to etch. In enameling, a soluble compound that helps control the suspension of glass powder in liquid-form enamels.

Enameling iron. Ultra-low-carbon steel alloy specifically developed for enameling.

Etchant. Chemical solution that causes metal to etch.

Expander. Machine which uses a pressured slitting and stretching process to transform solid metal sheets and coils into expanded metal.

F

Firing temperature. In enameling, the temperature at which glass enamel fuses.

Flexible shaft machine, flex shaft, flexshaft. A tool system used by jewelers consisting of a rotary motor and a handpiece that can hold many attachments.

Flux. Chemical agent that aids in soldering or fusing metal by removing oxide films from the surface, causing solder or fused metals to flow more uniformly.

Fusion. Process of melting separate elements into a unified whole.

G

Galvanic corrosion. Electrochemical process where one metal corrodes when it is in contact with another and an electrolyte such as water or sweat is present.

Galvanized steel. Steel that has a protective coating of zinc to prevent rusting. When heated, zinc fumes are released, which are toxic to breathe.

Gauge. Value that identifies the thickness of sheet metals. The higher the number, the thinner the metal.

Goat and sheep hoof trimmer. Multi-purpose hand shear designed to trim the hooves of goats, sheep and alpaca. Sharp enough to cut up to 18 gauge cold rolled low carbon steel.

Grip coat. See ground coat.

Ground coat. Liquid enamel undercoat containing metal oxides that promote the bonding of steel and enamels.

Guillotine shear. Shear that consists of a blade that moves up and down and a bed that the metal is placed on held down by a clamp or hold-down device. Guillotine shears cut metals with high precision and accuracy. They are also known as squaring shears and cutting shears.

H

Hot rolled steel. Steel that has been rolled at a high temperature (over 1700°F/927°C). It is easy to form but has a less refined surface than cold rolled steel.

Hydraulic press. Machine with a strong steel frame and hydraulic cylinder that generates a compressive force to perform a wide range of metal forming and fabrication processes.

I

Industrial enamel. See liquid enamel.

K

Karat. Measure of the fineness (i.e., purity) of gold. It is spelled carat outside the U.S. (not to be confused with the unit used to measure the weight of gems, also called carat).

Keum Boo. Ancient Korean technique used to bond sheets of metal foil (gold, silver or alloys of the two) to silver, steel and other metals. The bond is established through a process called solid state diffusion involving atomic exchange between the metals.

L

Liquid enamel, liquid-form enamel. Mixture of enamel, water, clay and electrolytes that is applied in liquid form, dried and fired to steel and other metals.

Liquid state diffusion. Movement of a liquid from an area of higher concentration to an area of lower concentration until the molecules are evenly distributed.

Low carbon steel. Steel that has 0.04–0.3% carbon. The most common grade of carbon steel.

M

Matte finish. Smooth even surface free from shine or highlights.

Metal cloth. Mesh sheet comprised of fine woven metallic wire.

Mild steel. A type of low carbon steel with 0.05–0.25% carbon.

Mordant. See etchant.

N

Neutral flame. Flame with a balanced oxygen-fuel ratio. Color is semi-transparent purple or blue and is optimal for many uses because it does not oxidize.

Neutralize. Make chemically neutral (neither acid nor basic).

Nibblers. Electric hand shear with three blades that chop and remove a narrow strip of metal along the cutting line.

Noble metals. Group of metals that resist oxidation, corrosion and the effects of acids. The opposite of base metals, which more readily oxidize and corrode. Examples of noble metals include gold, silver and platinum.

O

Open work, piercing. Metal that has been sawed, pressed or punched to create decorative holes.

Oxidizing flame. Flame having an excess of oxygen (as the outer cone of a gas flame). The flame shortens due to quicker combustion, its color becomes a more transparent blue, and it hisses.

P

Pickle. Liquid compound, which usually contains an acid, used to remove oxidation, impurities, stains, rust, scale and flux from soldered or fused metals.

Porcelain enamel. See liquid enamel.

Power shears. Shears that are either electrically or pneumatically powered and operated by hand. Ideal for cutting large pieces of sheet metal.

Q

Quench. Submerge hot metal into a water bath to cool it quickly.

R

Recycled steel. Steel that is converted into reusable material. Steel is 100 percent recyclable into material of the same quality.

Reducing atmosphere. Condition characterized by the absence of oxygen which prevents oxidation. Can be produced in a kiln by burying the metal in charcoal, which creates carbon monoxide that absorbs the oxygen.

Resist. In etching metals, a material that is applied to the metal surface to block the action of the etchant as it dissolves metal particles in the exposed areas.

S

SAE. Society of Automotive Engineers, now known as SAE International; maintains a grading standard used to designate the strength of steel primarily for use in the automotive and aerospace industry. The system has four grades—A, B, C and D—with A being the weakest and D being the strongest.

Scale. Flaky surface of hot rolled steel, consisting of mixed iron oxides.

Sgraffito. Mark making technique in enameling where lines or marks are drawn into dry unfired enamel, exposing the layer underneath, whether this be bare metal, ground coat, or a previously enameled layer.

Slag. Stony waste matter separated from metals during the refining of ore.

Smelting. Process of applying heat and a chemical reducing agent to an ore to extract desired metals such as iron, copper, silver, tin, lead and zinc.

Solid state diffusion. Process where the atoms of two solid metals intersperse over time.

T

Throatless shear. Shear used to make straight and curved cuts in sheet metal. Sheet metal can be fed past the angle where the blades converge and moved around the cutting blades allowing great flexibility in cutting angles, curves and shapes.

Tin snip. General class of hand shear typically with a long handle, short blades and wide jaws. A simple tin snip consists of handles attached to jaws and joined by a pin at the center. Compound snips are often called aviation snips. See aviation snip.

V

Virgin steel. Steel that is manufactured using basic oxygen furnaces (BOFs) which burn coal to smelt ore, extracting the iron.

Vitreous enamel. In enameling, a fine ground glass that is applied to a metal in powder form and fired.

W

Wet process enamel. See liquid enamel.

Work harden. Strengthen and harden a metal by deformation, such as hammering or rolling in a mill.

INDEX

A SPECIAL THANKS

Artisan Ideas would like to extend our thanks to Harold O'Connor for his assistance in looking over some of the technical aspects of this book.

Harold O'Connor has been a practicing metalsmith for over 50 years. Educated in the United States, Germany, Finland, Denmark and Austria, he has conducted workshops in over 300 schools over North America and in 23 countries abroad, including South Korea, New Zealand, Peru, and Estonia. His work is in many private and public collections including The Metropolitan Museum of Art in New York City, the Smithsonian in Washington D.C., the Victoria and Albert Museum in London, the Boston Museum of Fine Art, and The Racine Art Museum in Wisconsin.

He is the author of two books: *The Jeweler's Bench Reference* and *The Flexibleshaft Machine*, and also the DVD *Metalsmithing Techniques with Harold O'Connor*.